Railway World SPECIAL

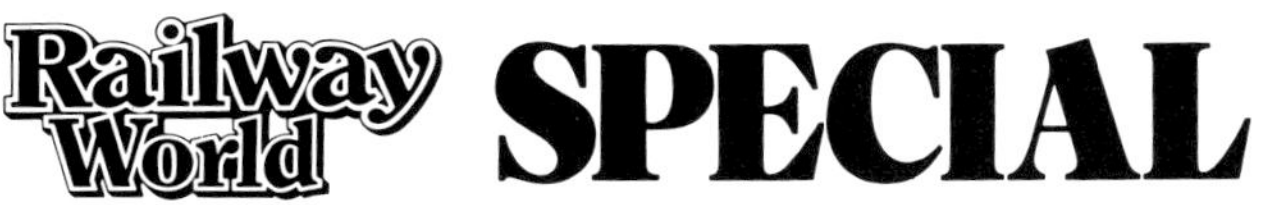

'CORNISH RIVIERA'

AF469184

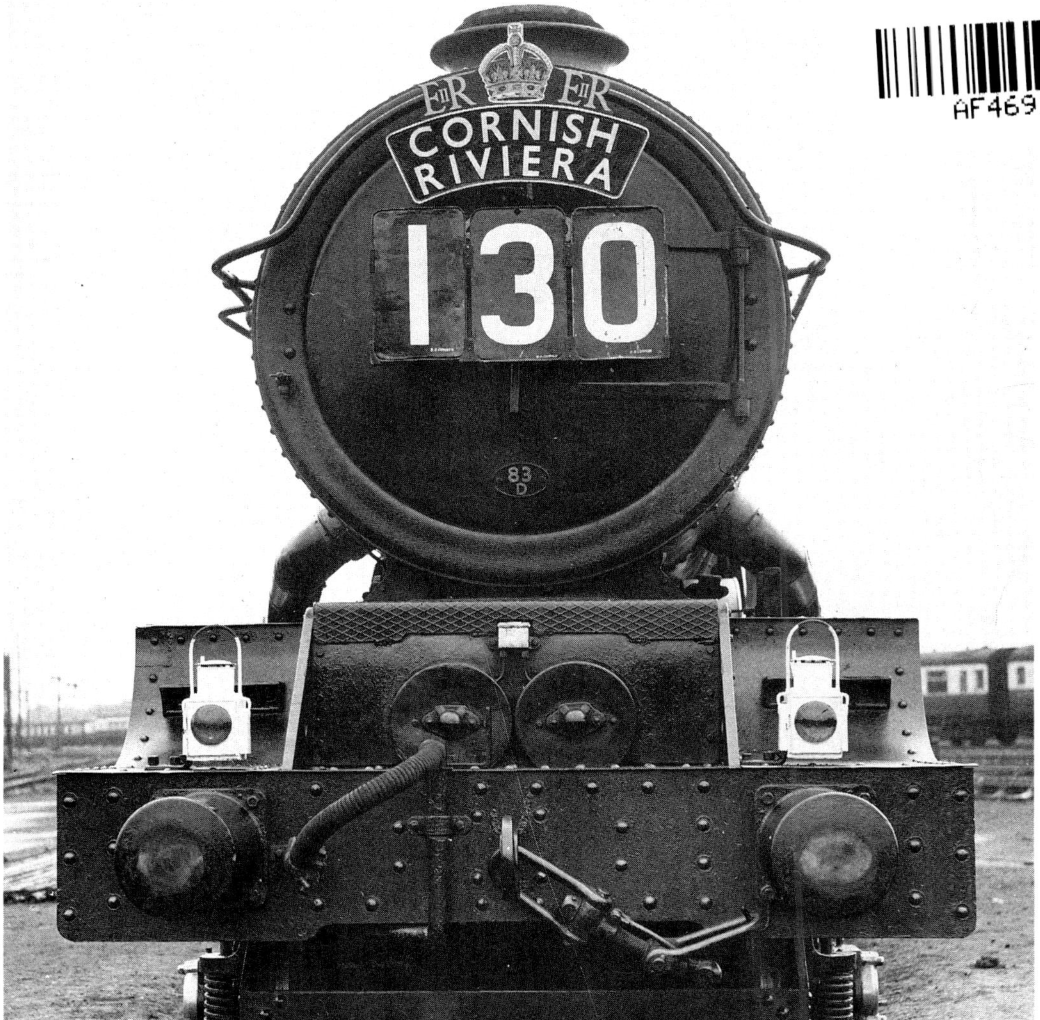

CHRIS LEIGH

LONDON
IAN ALLAN LTD

Contents

Above:
The new 'Centenary' coaching stock is featured in this official 1935 view of 'King' No 6002 *King William IV* heading the 'Cornish Riviera' through Teignmouth. *GWR*

Previous page:
The official portrait of a Laira-based 'King' wearing the special 'Cornish Riviera' headboard carried in 1953 to mark the Coronation of HM Queen Elizabeth II. *BR*

First published 1988

ISBN 0 7110 1797 2

All rights reserved. No part of this book may be reproduced or transmitted in any form or by any means, electronic or mechanical, including photo-copying, recording or by any information storage and retrieval system, without permission from the Publisher in writing.

© Ian Allan Ltd 1988

Published by Ian Allan Ltd, Shepperton, Surrey; and printed by Ian Allan Printing Ltd at their works at Coombelands in Runnymede, England

Front cover:
The 'Cornish Riviera' was not distinguished by a locomotive headboard until after Nationalisation in 1948. This is how the train looked in the first application of BR livery, with the locomotive in blue and the ex-GWR coaches in carmine and cream. 'King' 4-6-0 No 6025 *King Henry III* is seen at speed with the down train, west of Maidenhead, in the early 1950s.
From a painting by George Heiron

Back cover:
Led by power car No 43150, the up 'Cornish Riviera' climbs past Respryn Bridge towards Bodmin Parkway on 2 July 1987. *J. E. Oxley*

Preface

The 'Cornish Riviera' is not a new subject for a book. Over the years a number of publications have been devoted to the story of the Great Western Railway's prestige express, some of them by the most eminent of railway authors. I cannot count myself in the same league as messrs C. J. Allen and O. S. Nock, not least because they had the advantage of being able to ride on and record the 'Cornish Riviera' in its heyday, while I was born too late for that and can only imagine the thrill.

Therefore, and because of my railway modelling background, I have kept away from the locomotive performance and train timing angles so well documented elsewhere, and contented myself to provide an overview of the train and its history. I have endeavoured to concentrate on the changing appearance of the train and to put across a little of the atmosphere that surrounded it. I hope, too, that I have been able to show the importance of the part played by the Great Western Railway and by the 'Cornish Riviera' in establishing the Cornish coast as Britain's foremost holiday venue.

Left:
No D600 *Active*, first of the North British A1A-A1A diesel-hydraulics, sports the final style of headboard, introduced in the mid-1950s for steam locomotives.
John Maltby

CHAPTER ONE

Introduction

Cornwall is a county of mystique and legend. Its remote moors and rugged coastline have a magnetic appeal. Its reputation as a land of romance and adventure has been enhanced through countless books set against its rugged and sometimes harsh backcloth. From King Arthur and his Knights of the Round Table, popularly thought to be set around Tintagel, to the feuding gentry of 'Poldark', generations have been regaled with descriptions of the county.

Surrounded on three sides by sea, and almost severed from the rest of England by the River Tamar, Cornwall is unique in its geography and customs. Much of it a plateau of high moorland which drops steeply into the sea over granite cliffs, its fortunes were founded upon agriculture. Its mild climate provides a good growing season which enables earlier planting and harvesting of crops than is possible in most of the UK.

Discovery of metal ores, particularly tin, in surface deposits revealed in rivers and streams, led to the development of the mining industry. As it became necessary to pursue the valuable tin lodes deeper and deeper under ground, Cornwall was able to seize on the early benefits of the industrial revolution, using steam engines to pump water from the mines. Primitive railways and plateways transported the ore but the stationary pumping engines in their gaunt engine houses were the single biggest manifestation of industry in the county.

At the height of the mining era, more than 300 engine houses dotted the county, enabling ore to be recovered from deep underground shafts, and in some cases, from under the sea. Increasing imports of cheaper overseas ore and the rising cost of mining the increasingly inaccessible Cornish ore led to a sharp decline during the latter years of the 19th century. By the late 1890s many mines were abandoned, their stripped and derelict engine houses remaining to this day as a stark reminder of one-time prosperity.

The Cornish people had been fishermen for centuries and despite the rugged and ruthless coastline and the wild Atlantic storms, the valuable mackerel shoals had always been a vital resource. Those picture-postcard fishing villages such as Polperro, Mevagissey, Mousehole, and Coverack, whose granite-built cottages seem to tumble down the cliffs to the sea, were the points from which the fishermen set out to harvest this 'crop'. Mackerel is extremely perishable and most of the catch would be sold locally. This aspect of the industry was to change from the mid-19th century. The opening of 26 miles of standard gauge railway from Truro to Penzance by the West Cornwall Railway in 1852 heralded that change. Converted to mixed gauge and linked to the broad gauge Cornwall Railway, which opened its line over the Royal Albert Bridge at Saltash in 1859, the railway linked the western

Below:
Cornwall's 'Riviera'. An early 20th century view of St Ives with the fishing village and harbour seen from Porthminster Beach. The station is on the left above the retaining wall. Note the narrow gauge railway on the beach, worked by horses and used for shipping sand. *Real Photographs*

Left:
The type of poster used to put over the 'Riviera' message.

extremity of Cornwall with the rest of the UK.

Suddenly it became possible to send the fish catches further afield and as early as 1861 the first through fish traffic from Penzance to London was being recorded. By 1868 as much as 115 tons was being shipped in a single night, this being the catch from Newlyn, the fishing harbour close by Penzance station. In order to speed the transport process, a steamer was employed from 1869 to bring the catch in to Penzance from the boats, while they remained on the fishing grounds.

By 1879 traffic of all types at Penzance station had outgrown existing facilities and work commenced on construction of a new station. The cost was to be £26,000, including £4,000 for granite and another £4,000 for the train shed roof. The result was a fine terminus in a prominent location in the town, which stands largely unaltered to the present day.

Above:
Once the symbol of Cornish prosperity, a derelict engine house stands silent sentinel at Scorrier as No 50048 *Dauntless* hustles the up 'Cornish Riviera' past on 20 July 1978.
B. Morrison

At Newlyn the south pier of the harbour was extended by 700ft in 1885, the work costing £20,000. Continued growth in the fishing industry led to further extensions of the north pier in 1888 and 1894, totalling 1,760ft and costing £32,000. Newlyn was by far the busiest of the Cornish fishing harbours, and in 1919 took 31% of the total West Country catch. St Ives, also rail-served, was at this time taking 20%. By 1938 Newlyn's share was up to 51% while that of St Ives had fallen to 3%.

After World War 2, increasing intrusions by foreign fishing vessels and the departure of the staple shoals led to a sharp decline in Cornish fishing. The railway no longer carried fish and in 1987 Newlyn harbour, though still with an active fishing fleet,

TRAIN DEPARTURE

	TIME		PLATFORM	PRINCIPAL STATIONS SERVED
❸	4 a.m.	12	5	All Stations to Hayes.
❸	5 a.m.	10	5	All Stations to Uxbridge (except Staines Branch and Cowley). (Change at Ealing for Stations to Greenford).
		30 SX	3	Reading, Didcot, Swindon, Chippenham, Bath, Bristol, Bridgwater, Durston, Taunton, Wellington, Exeter, Dawlish, Teignmouth, Newton Abbot, Totnes, Brent, Plymouth and principal Stations to Penzance. *ON TUESDAYS ONLY also calls at Tiverton Junction.* (Change at Reading for Stations to Cholsey; at Didcot for Stations to Shrivenham; principal Stations to Birmingham, Wolverhampton and Stratford-upon-Avon, also the Worcester Line; at Swindon for Gloucester Line; at Chippenham for Westbury and Weymouth Line; at Bristol for South Wales; and at Taunton for Minehead, Barnstaple and Ilfracombe).
		30 SO	3	Reading, Didcot, Swindon, Chippenham, Bath, Bristol, Weston-super-Mare, Highbridge, Bridgwater, Durston, Taunton and Minehead. (Change at Reading for Stations to Cholsey; at Didcot for Stations to Shrivenham; principal Stations to Birmingham, Wolverhampton and Stratford-upon-Avon, also the Worcester Line; at Swindon for Gloucester Line; at Chippenham for Westbury and Weymouth Line; and at Bristol for South Wales).
		42	4	All Stations to Windsor (except Staines Branch). (Change at Ealing for Stations to Greenford).
	6 a.m.	5	5	All Stations to Uxbridge (except Staines Branch). (Change at Ealing for Stations to Greenford).
		25	1	West Drayton, Slough, Maidenhead, Twyford, Reading and Stations to Didcot. (Change at West Drayton for Uxbridge Branch; at Slough for Windsor; at Twyford for Henley Branch; and at Reading for Stations to Basingstoke *and on SATURDAYS ONLY for Stations to Newbury*).
		30	15	Ealing, Southall and Stations to Slough Depot (except Staines Branch). *(ON SATURDAYS terminates at SLOUGH).* (Change at Ealing for Stations to Greenford and at Slough for Burnham, Taplow, Maidenhead and Stations to High Wycombe). (Change at Bourne End for Marlow).
		33	§ 3	All Stations to Slough Depot (except Uxbridge Branch).
		38	4	All Stations to Uxbridge (except Staines Branch). *(ON SATURDAYS ONLY change at Ealing for Stations to Greenford).*
		48 SX	§ 3	All Stations to Hayes. (Change at Ealing for Stations to Greenford).
		55 SO	3	(SATURDAYS, 3rd JULY to 21st AUGUST, INCLUSIVE). Pymouth, Liskeard, Bodmin Road, Par and principal Stations to Penzance. (Change at Liskeard for Looe and at Par for Newquay).
R	7 a.m.	0 SO	5	(SATURDAYS, 26th JUNE to 21st AUGUST, INCLUSIVE). Taunton, Exeter, Dawlish, Teignmouth, Newton Abbot, Torre, Torquay, Paignton, Churston (for Brixham) and Kingswear. (Change at Taunton for Minehead, Barnstaple and Ilfracombe).
		5 SX	5	Ealing, Slough and Windsor. (Change at Slough for Burnham, Taplow, Maidenhead and Twyford). (Connects at Twyford for Henley Branch).
		10 SX	1	Reading, Didcot, Oxford, Banbury, Leamington Spa, Birmingham and Wolverhampton. (Change at Reading for Stations to Devizes; and at Leamington Spa for Stratford-upon-Avon and Stations to Bordesley).
		10 SO	1	Ealing, Slough, Reading, Didcot, Oxford, Banbury, Leamington Spa, Birmingham and Wolverhampton. (Change at Ealing for Stations to Greenford; at Slough for Windsor and Stations to Twyford (change for Henley Branch); and at Leamington for Stratford-upon-Avon and Stations to Bordesley).
		12 SX	15	All Stations to Uxbridge (except Staines Branch). (Change at Ealing for Stations to Greenford).
		15 SO	3	(SATURDAYS, 19th and 26th JUNE, also SATURDAYS, 28th AUGUST to 18th SEPTEMBER, INCLUSIVE). Newbury, Frome, Taunton, Exeter, Teignmouth, Newton Abbot, Pymouth, Liskeard and principal Stations to Penzance. (Change at Frome for Yeovil, Maiden Newton, Dorchester and Weymouth, and at Taunton for Barnstaple).
		20 SO	5	All Stations to West Drayton; Slough, Burnham, Taplow, Maidenhead and Twyford. (Connects at Twyford for Henley Branch).
		25 SX	§ 4	All Stations to Southall; Slough, Burnham, Taplow, Maidenhead and Twyford. (Connects at Twyford for Henley Branch).
R		30 SX	1	Reading, Didcot, Swindon, Chippenham, Corsham, Bath, Bristol, Bridgwater, Taunton, Exeter, Dawlish, Teignmouth, Newton Abbot, Kingskerswell, Torre, Torquay and Paignton. (Change at Reading for Stations to Newbury; at Didcot for Stations to Oxford; and at Swindon for Gloucester Line and Cheltenhm Spa; and at Taunton for Minehead).
R		30 SO	1	Reading, Didcot, Swindon, Chippenham, Corsham, Bath, Bristol, Bridgwater, Taunton, Exeter and Starcross. (Change at Reading for Stations to Newbury; at Didcot for Stations to Oxford; at Swindon for Gloucester Line and Cheltenham Spa; at Bristol for Weston-super-Mare and at Taunton for Minehead).
		33 SX	3	All Stations to Hayes.
		36	§ 4	Ealing, Hayes, West Drayton, Iver, Langley, Slough, Taplow, Maidenhead and Stations to Bourne End, High Wycombe, Princes Risborough, Thame and Oxford. (Change at Ealing for Stations to Greenford; at West Drayton for Uxbridge and Staines Branches; at Slough for Windsor and at Bourne End for Marlow).
		40 SO	3	(SATURDAYS, 10th JULY to 28th AUGUST, INCLUSIVE). Torquay and Paignton.
		50	5	All Stations to Langley (except Staines Branch). (Change at Ealing for Stations to Greenford).
		55 SO	1	(SATURDAYS, 17th JULY to 14th AUGUST, INCLUSIVE). Newport, Cardiff, Bridgend, Port Talbot, Neath, Swansea and Stations to Carmarthen.
	8 a.m.	0 SX	1	REAR PORTION:—Ealing, Slough, Maidenhead, Reading and Stations to Oxford. (Change at Slough for Windsor, at Maidenhead for Twyford (change for Henley Branch) and at Reading for Basingstoke). FRONT PORTION:—Reading, Didcot, Oxford and Banbury. (Change at Oxford for principal Stations to Worcester, Malvern and Hereford and for Stations to Kings Sutton).
		0 SO	4	Ealing, Slough, Maidenhead, Reading and Stations to Didcot; Oxford, Banbury, Leamington Spa, Birmingham and Wolverhampton. (Change at Slough for Windsor, Burnham and Taplow; at Maidenhead for Twyford (change for Henley); at Reading for Stations to Basingstoke; and at Oxford for principal Stations to Worcester, Malvern and Hereford).
		10 SO	5	(SATURDAYS, 19th JUNE to 4th SEPTEMBER, INCLUSIVE). Teignmouth, Newton Abbot Torquay and Paignton. (Change at Newton Abbot for Moretonhampstead).
		15 SX	4	Ealing, Southall, West Drayton, Slough and Maidenhead.
		15 SO	15	Ealing, Hayes and Slough. (Connects at Slough for Windsor).
		18	14	All Stations to Uxbridge. (Change at Ealing for Stations to Greenford and *ON SATURDAYS ONLY at West Drayton for Staines Branch).*
R		20 SX	3	Westbury, Yeovil (Pen Mill) and Weymouth Quay (FOR THE CHANNEL ISLANDS). (Change at Westbury for Trowbridge, Frome, Castle Cary, Maiden Newton, Dorchester and Weymouth Town and at Yeovil (Pen Mill) for Yeovil (Town) and Stations to Athelney).
R		20 SO	3	(SATURDAYS, 19th JUNE to 11th SEPTEMBER, INCLUSIVE). Weymouth Quay (FOR THE CHANNEL ISLANDS).
R		25 SO	1	(SATURDAYS, 19th JUNE to 4th SEPTEMBER, INCLUSIVE). Brent, Plymouth, Liskeard and principal Stations to Perranporth and Penzance. (Change at Brent for Kingsbridge).
R		30 SO	4	Weymouth Quay (FOR THE CHANNEL ISLANDS).
		35 SX	5	Ealing, Hayes, West Drayton and Slough. (Connects at Slough for Windsor). (Change at Ealing for Stations to Greenford and at West Drayton for Staines Branch).
R		40 SO	5	Reading, Newport, Cardiff, Port Talbot, Neath, Swansea, Llanelly, Whitland, Narberth, Tenby and Pembroke Dock.
R		45 SX	3	"THE BRISTOLIAN." Bristol only.
		48	14	All Stations to Windsor (except Uxbridge and Staines Branches). (Change at Ealing for Stations to Greenford).
R		50 SX	1	Newport Cardiff, Port Talbot, Neath, Swansea, Llanelly, Whitland, Narberth, Tenby and Pembroke Dock.
R		50 SO	1	Exeter, Dawlish, Teignmouth, Newton Abbot, Torquay and Paignton.
R		55	2	Reading, Newport, Cardiff, Bridgend, Port Talbot, Neath, Swansea, Llanelly, Carmarthen, St. Clears, Whitland and Stations to Pembroke Dock; Clynderwen, Clarbeston Road, Haverfordwest, Johnston and Neyland. (Change at Reading for Newbury, Devizes and Trowbridge, also for Stations to Didcot and at Johnston for Milford Haven).
R	9 a.m.	0 SX	4	"THE INTER-CITY." Birmingham and Wolverhampton.
R		0 SO	4	(SATURDAYS, 19th JUNE to 11th SEPTEMBER, INCLUSIVE). Birmingham, Wolverhampton, Shrewsbury, Ruabon, Barmouth, Harlech, Portmadoc, Criccieth, Afon Wen, Penychain (for Pwllheli Holiday Camp) and Pwllheli. (Change at Ruabon for Llangollen and Bala).
R		5 SX	5	Reading, Bath and Bristol. (Connects for Stations to Weston-super-Mare).
R		5 SO	5	Reading, Chippenham, Bath, Bristol, Yatton and Weston-super-Mare. (Change at Chippenham for Trowbridge and at Bristol for Stations to Durston).
R		10	3	High Wycombe, Bicester, Banbury, Leamington Spa, Stratford-upon-Avon, Birmingham, Wolverhampton, Wellington (Salop), Shrewsbury, Gobowen, Ruabon, Wrexham, Chester, Hooton, Rock Ferry and Birkenhead. (Change at High Wycombe for Stations to Princes Risborough, Watlington and King's Sutton; at Gobowen for Oswestry and at Ruabon for Barmouth and Pwllheli).
R		15	1	Reading, Didcot, Swindon, Gloucester Line, Cheltenham Spa, Ross-on-Wye, Monmouth and Hereford; Chippenham, Bath, Bristol and Stations to Durston, also EXCEPT ON SATURDAYS to Taunton. (Change at Reading for Stations to Basingstoke and Cholsey; *also on SATURDAYS ONLY for Theale and Stations to Newbury*; at Didcot for Stations to Oxford and Shrivenham and at Chippenham (EXCEPT ON SATURDAYS for Trowbridge).
		20	15	Ealing, Southall, Hayes, West Drayton, Slough, Burnham, Taplow, Maidenhead and Stations to High Wycombe, Princes Risborough, Thame and Oxford. (Change at West Drayton for Uxbridge Branch; at Slough for Windsor; at Maidenhead for Twyford (change for Henley Branch); at Bourne End for Marlow and at Princes Risborough for Aylesbury).
R		30 SX	2	Reading, Newbury, Taunton, Exeter, Newton Abbot, Plymouth and principal Stations to Newquay and Falmouth. Change at Reading for Theale and Stations to Thatcham; at Taunton for Minehead; at Newton Abbot for Stations to Kingswear and at Liskeard for Looe).
R		30 SO	2	Plymouth, Par and Newquay. *(ON SATURDAYS, 11th and 18th SEPTEMBER also calls at Brent (for Kingsbridge)).*
		33	14	All Stations to Slough (except Uxbridge and Staines). (Change at Ealing for Stations to Greenford).
		35 SO	4	(SATURDAYS, 19th JUNE to 11th SEPTEMBER, INCLUSIVE). Westbury, Taunton and Minehead. (Change at Westbury for Trowbridge, Frome, Castle Cary, Yeovil, Maiden Newton, Dorchester and Weymouth and at Taunton for Barnstaple and Ilfracombe and Stations to Dunster).
		40 SO	3	(SATURDAYS, 19th JUNE to 4th SEPTEMBER, INCLUSIVE). Newton Abbot, Torquay and Paignton. (Change at Newton Abbot for Moretonhampstead).
R		45	1	Reading, Didcot, Oxford, Kingham, Moreton-in-Marsh, Honeybourne, Evesham, Worcester, Malvern and Hereford; and EXCEPT ON SATURDAYS Banbury, Leamington Spa and Birmingham. (Change at Reading for Stations to Cholsey; at Didcot for Stations to Radley (for Abingdon); at Kingham for Chipping Norton and Stations to Cheltenham Spa; at Evesham for Pershore and at Worcester for Kidderminster and Stourbridge).
		55 SO	5	(SATURDAYS, 17th JULY to 28th AUGUST, INCLUSIVE). Newport, Cardiff, Bridgend, Port Talbot, Neath, Swansea, Llanelly, Carmarthen, St. Clears, Whitland, Clynderwen, Clarbeston Road, Haverfordwest, Johnston and Neyland. (Change at Whitland for Cardigan and at Johnston for Milford Haven).
	10 a.m.	0 SX	5	Ealing, Hayes, West Drayton, Iver, Langley, Slough, Burnham, Taplow, Maidenhead, Twyford and Reading. (Change at West Drayton for Uxbridge and Staines Branches; at Slough for Windsor; at Twyford for Henley Branch *and on SATURDAYS ONLY at Maidenhead for Stations to High Wycombe). (Change at Bourne End for Marlow).*
		0 SO	14	
		7	15	All Stations to Uxbridge.
R		10 SX	3	"CAMBRIAN COAST EXPRESS." Banbury, Birmingham, Wolverhampton, Shrewsbury, Welshpool, Newtown, Moat Lane Junction, Machynlleth, Borth, Aberystwyth; Aberdovey, Towyn, Barmouth and Pwllheli.
		15 SO	1	Oxford, Heyford, Banbury, Leamington Spa, Birmingham and Wolverhampton. (Change at Oxford for Handborough and Stations to Chipping Norton).
		20 SO	5	Torquay, Paignton, Goodrington Sands Halt, Churston (for Brixham) and Kingswear.
R K		30 SX	2	"CORNISH RIVIERA EXPRESS." Westbury (Slip) for Weymouth Line; Plymouth, Par, Truro, Gwinear Road, St. Erth and Penzance. (Change at Par for Newquay; at Truro for Falmouth Branch and Stations to Camborne, Hayle and Marazion; at Gwinear Road for Helston and at St. Erth for St. Ives).
R		30 SO	2	"CORNISH RIVIERA EXPRESS." Truro, St. Erth, Lelant, Carbis Bay, St. Ives and Penzance.
R		35 SO	3	Plymouth, Truro, Falmouth, Gwinear Road and Penzance. (Change at Gwinear Road for Helston).
		42	15	All Stations to Slough (except Staines Branch). (Change at Ealing for Stations to Greenford).
R		[illegible]	1	Reading, Didcot, Swindon, Kemble, Chalford, Stroud, Gloucester and Cheltenham Spa. (Change at Reading for Newbury, Kintbury, Hungerford, and EXCEPT ON SATURDAYS for Stations to Trowbridge; at Didcot EXCEPT ON SATURDAYS for Stations to Oxford; at Kemble for Cirencester and Tetbury and at Gloucester for Ross-on-Wye, Monmouth and Hereford).
R		50 SO	2	"CAMBRIAN COAST EXPRESS." Banbury, Leamington Spa, Birmingham, Wolverhampton, Welshpool, Newtown, Machynlleth, Borth, Aberystwyth, Aberdovey, Towyn, Fairbourne, Barmouth, Harlech, Portmadoc, Criccieth, Penychain (for Pwllheli Holiday Camp) and Pwllheli. (Connects at Barmouth Junction for Dolgelley).
R		[illegible]	5	"THE PEMBROKE COAST EXPRESS." Newport, Cardiff, Swansea, Llanelly, Carmarthen, St. Clears, Whitland, Tenby and Pembroke Dock. (Connects at Whitland for Neyland).

SUSPENSION OF, OR ALTERATION TO, TRAIN SERVICES

The train services and other facilities shewn in this departure sheet are subject to alteration or cancellation at short notice and do not necessarily apply on Bank or other Public Holidays or on Race Days.

SX—SATURDAYS EXCEPTED SO—SATURDAYS ONLY ❸—THIRD CLASS ONLY.

§—Trains so marked usually stand with another Train at the same Platform. Passengers must enquire for their correct Train.

R—Refreshment Car Train K—Passengers travelling in Slip Carriages cannot obtain access to Refreshment Cars.

showed little of the bustle of earlier days, its catch being sent by road in refrigerated lorries, the fish packed in plywood boxes made in Russia!

By the turn of the century many of the smaller harbours had been unable to keep pace with the dramatic expansion of the fishing industry, and without rail connection they could not take advantage of rapid transit to markets outside the county. Fishing harbours such as Sennen, Mousehole and Polperro thus diminished in importance as the rail-linked ports grew, but the declining harbours were to take on a new significance.

These quaint and picturesque locations, with their tales of smugglers, wreckers and sea-faring folk possessed many of the virtues that the British find so appealing. The wide availability of prints, lithographs and artists' impressions enabled town and city dwellers from far afield to appreciate the delights of Cornwall. In the final quarter of the 19th century the Great Western Railway acquired full control of the separate companies which had controlled its route to Cornwall; the Bristol & Exeter, South Devon, Cornwall, and West Cornwall Railways. A range of through tickets could then be offered to tempt the tourist and holidaymaker to Cornwall.

The mild climate, which encouraged the growth of distinctive sub-tropical plants and trees, and the similarity of the whitewashed stone villages to some of those on the Mediterranean led to inevitable comparisons with continental resorts. It was to be the Great Western Railway which christened Cornwall 'England's Riviera' and whose vigorous publicity department did so much to promote the county as a premier holiday location. It was in the summer of 1904 that the GWR launched a new non-stop express train from Paddington to Plymouth and then principal stations to Penzance, with a start-to-finish timing of just 7hr, and christened it the 'Cornish Riviera Express'.

Above:
The 'Cornish Riviera' of the 1980s formed by an IC125 unit lays a haze over West Drayton station on the final leg of its journey from Penzance, with Paddington just a few more minutes away. The date is 13 June 1987. *B. Morrison*

Left:
Part of the poster timetable display from Paddington for a summer in the late 1950s. The 'Cornish Riviera' weekday and Saturday details are shown, together with numerous stations no longer in the timetable. *Author's Collection*

Below:
Examples of 'Cornish Riviera' timetables; 1958 and 1959.

Table 3

CORNISH RIVIERA EXPRESS

RESTAURANT CAR SERVICE

LONDON, PLYMOUTH, TRURO and PENZANCE

WEEK DAYS and SUNDAYS

	E	S	SUNS.
	am	am	am
London (Paddington) dep	10A30	10A30	10A30
	pm		pm
Plymouth (North Rd.). arr	2 30	..	3 25
Par.. .. .. "	3 32	..	..
		pm	
Truro .. .. "	4 3	4 28	5 0
Redruth .. "	..	..	5 22
Camborne .. "	..	..	5 32
Gwinear Road "	4 33	..	..
St. Erth .. "	4 43	5 12	5 48
Penzance .. "	4 55	5 25	6 0

	E	S	SUNS.
	am	am	am
Penzance .. dep	10A 0	10B 0	9A45
St. Erth .. "	10A10	..	9A55
Gwinear Road "	10A22	10B22	..
Camborne .. "	..	..	10 11
Truro .. .. "	10 52	10 52	10 38
Par.. .. .. "	11 22	..	11 10
	pm	pm	pm
Plymouth (North Rd.) "	12A30	12A30	12A20
Exeter (St. David's) "	..	..	1 50
London (Paddington) arr	4 40	5 20	5 30

A—Seats can be reserved in advance on payment of a fee of 2s. 0d. per seat (see page 22).
B—Passengers travelling beyond Plymouth are required to hold Regulation Tickets (see page 31), see also Note "A".
E—Except Saturdays. S—Saturdays only.

CORNISH RIVIERA EXPRESS

RESTAURANT CAR SERVICE (¶)

LONDON, PLYMOUTH, TRURO and PENZANCE

(Also conveys through carriages to Torquay, Paignton and Kingswear and on Weekdays from Kingswear, Paignton and Torquay—see Table 81)

WEEK DAYS and SUNDAYS

	WEEK DAYS	SUNS.
	am	am
London (Paddington) dep	10A30	10A30
Reading General .. "	..	11 15
	pm	pm
Westbury .. .. arr	..	12 20
Taunton .. .. "	12 47	1 20
Exeter (St. David's) "	1 22	2 0
Newton Abbot .. "	2 1	2 32
Torre .. .. .. "	..	2 55
Torquay .. .. "	2 15	3 0
Paignton .. .. "	2 25	3 10
Churston (for Brixham) .. "	2 36	3 21
Kingswear .. .. "	2 45	3 30
Plymouth .. .. .. "	2 45	3 30
Liskeard .. .. .. "	..	4 11
Par .. .. .. "	3 44	4 39
St. Austell .. .. "	..	4 52
Truro .. .. .. "	4 13	5 16
Redruth .. .. .. "	4 33	5 38
Camborne .. .. "	..	5 47
Hayle .. .. .. "	..	5 58
St. Erth .. .. .. "	4 51	6 5
Penzance .. .. .. "	5 5	6 20

	WEEK DAYS	SUNS.
	am	am
Penzance .. .. dep	10A10	9A35
St. Erth .. .. "	10A21	9A45
Hayle .. .. "	..	9A52
Camborne .. .. "	..	10A 9
Redruth .. .. "	10A42	10A19
Truro .. .. "	11A 0	10A38
St. Austell .. .. "	..	11A 3
Par .. .. "	11A29	11A12
Lostwithiel .. .. "	..	11 22
Bodmin Road.. .. "	..	11 31
Liskeard .. .. "	..	11 50
	pm	pm
Plymouth .. .. "	12A30	12A30
Kingswear .. "	12A22	..
Churston (for Brixham) .. "	12A32	..
Paignton .. .. "	12A43	..
Torquay .. .. "	12A55	..
Newton Abbot .. "	1 10	..
Exeter (St. David's) "	1 58	2 0
Taunton .. .. "	2 34	2 39
London (Paddington) arr	4 54	5 25

A—Seats can be reserved in advance on payment of a fee of 2s. 0d. per seat (see page 49)
¶—Restaurant Car available between London (Paddington) and Plymouth (Weekdays), Newton Abbot (Sundays) and between Plymouth and London (Paddington) on Weekdays and Sundays

CHAPTER TWO

The Route

For its first two years the 'Cornish Riviera' followed the Great Western's main line route via Bath and Bristol to Taunton, the route which was christened the 'Great Way Round'. On 1 July 1906 the extension of the Berks & Hants route through Westbury to Castle Cary, was completed. It was this route which was to become the main line to Devon and Cornwall and accordingly, apart from emergency diversions, it became the regular route for the 'Cornish Riviera'.

The train would depart from platform 1 at Paddington, its maximum loading of 14 coaches causing the locomotive to stand towards the end of the platform, protruding into the narrow station throat, with the large black expanse of the goods station on one side, and high buildings on the other, giving a rather confined impression. The goods station was demolished in 1986, completely altering the character of the station throat.

On departure from Brunel's great terminus, the line passes under Bishops Road, and Ranelagh Bridge stabling point is seen to the left. Here there was a turntable, coaling and watering facilities which avoided the need for locomotives on quick turnrounds to travel down to Old Oak Common for servicing. The stabling point was squeezed into a very small site but nevertheless survived in use until the 1970s when the dwindling use of locomotives made its retention uneconomic.

The line is surrounded by light industry and scruffy suburbs, until on the north side of the line a vast expanse of sidings is revealed just before passing under the junctions at Acton. Here, on the right, is Old Oak Common depot, the miles of carriage sidings hiding the locomotive depot at their back. Beyond Old Oak, and on the same side of the line, was the large expanse of Acton Yard, the Great Western's principal London marshalling yard. Closed in the early 1980s, it is now wasteland with a few engineers' sidings and a distribution depot for Foster Yeoman stone trains. Ealing Broadway station provides connections with District and Central Line trains and is the first major station out of Paddington. The postwar reconstruction in concrete and glass has left not a vestige of the old GWR. At West Ealing the triangular junction of the branch to Greenford diverges northwards.

The first major engineering feature of the line is Brunel's Wharncliffe Viaduct over the River Brent, just west of Hanwell station. The remaining, much-rationalised buildings of the timber station at Hanwell have been restored, complete with imitation gas lamps, but an express such as the 'Cornish Riviera' is by now gathering speed and the station and viaduct are passed in a moment. Southall, nearly 10 miles out from Paddington is now the home of a preservation group with premises near the station, but the once busy locomotive shed, latterly a DMU depot, is now largely empty. A curious twist of fate will see it become a steam depot once again when certain preserved locomotives operating from Marylebone are based there. At West Drayton the branch lines to Uxbridge and Staines diverged on the north side of the main line. The Uxbridge line closed in 1962 and has since been lifted, but the remains of the Staines branch can be seen skirting round the coal concentration depot, to pass under the main line. The single track then heads southwards towards the M25 motorway but is blocked off beyond Thorney Mill sidings, where a Bardon Quarries road coatings plant has given this short section of the line a new lease of life.

Running at full speed the 'Cornish Riviera' slips through the wide cutting at Iver, where the M25 motorway now crosses the line, and passes Iver and Langley local stations before reaching Slough. The grand Great Western station here is the junction for the short branch to Windsor which diverges southwards, just beyond the station. The triangular junction with the branch has been removed, as have the engine shed and most of the goods sidings.

The River Thames is glimpsed briefly from Brunel's Maidenhead bridge and at Maidenhead station the truncated remains of the Wycombe Railway terminate in the

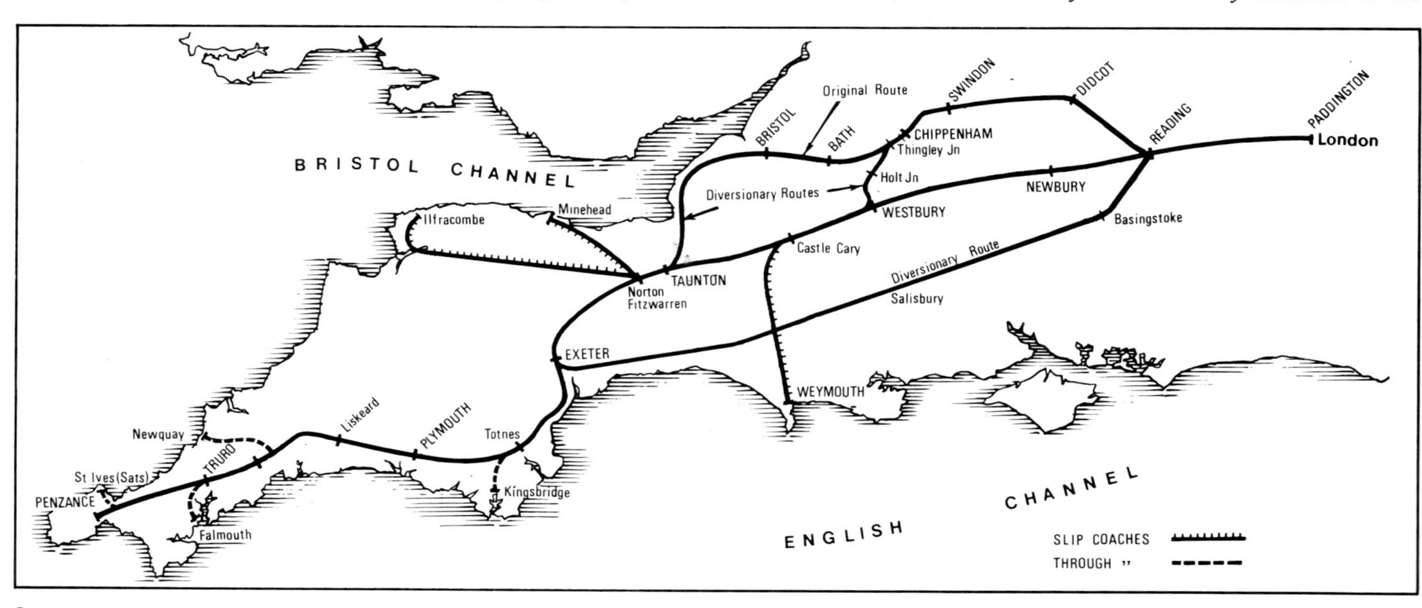

Above:
Paddington has never honoured the 'Cornish Riviera' with a special ticket barrier entrance as the Southern did with Pullman services like the 'Golden Arrow'. Instead, Platform one was an open platform and is seen here in the early 1930s at 10.15am. A '57xx' 0-6-0PT has brought in the stock for the down 'Cornish Riviera' and the 10.30 departure time is shown on the indicator, but there is otherwise nothing to identify the Railway's prestige express. *GWR*

Left:
A 1951 view, with pre-departure snacks — complete with Festival of Britain packaging — available from the platform trolley. The coach is one of the postwar GWR 'Hawksworth' vehicles in carmine and cream livery and providing a clear view of the carriage roofboard, now much more sensibly positioned below the gutters.
Ian Allan Library

train shed on the north side of the line. Once a through route to High Wycombe, this is now a branch line to Bourne End and Marlow. The scenery becomes more rural, interrupted only by Twyford station, where the branch to Henley diverges northwards immediately beyond the station. The train then enters Sonning Cutting where the 80ft deep gorge was dug by men and horses wallowing in the worst winter mud.

Emerging from the cutting, the train approaches the major station at Reading, currently the subject of massive reconstruction. The Southern line from Waterloo runs in on the left side to terminate, but all trace of the erstwhile Southern station has disappeared under office developments. Beyond Reading station the traditional route of the 'Cornish Riviera' diverges from Brunel's London-Bristol main line to take the 'Berks & Hants' route. It skirts the south

Above:
A splendid view from the cab of 'Western' No D1022 *Western Sentinel* about to roar, non-stop, through platform 4 at Reading General with the down 'Cornish Riviera' on 28 April 1970. At this time 'Westerns' were taking over from the twin 'Warship' lash-ups on the 'Cornish Riviera' and drivers were finding difficulty in keeping to the accelerated schedules. *G. P. Cooper*

Left:
A fine vantage point on the Berks & Hants line. The site of Savernake Low Level station is seen here on 13 June 1973, with the remains of the old Marlborough branch curving away to the right. No D1049 *Western Monarch* is passing on the up 'Cornish Riviera' formed of early Mk 2 coaches fitted with the waist level yellow destination plates. *J. H. Cooper-Smith*

Top right:
After passing through Wellington the line climbs to Whiteball tunnel. Leaving the tunnel and cresting the summit, 'King' No 6021 *King Richard II* heads the down 'Cornish Riviera' on 27 June 1953. *J. G. Hubback*

Centre right:
The original four-character headcode for the 'Cornish Riviera' was 1C30, here correctly displayed as the only identification on the front of 'Warship' B-B No D868 *Zephyr*. This is a Sunday working, seen on 25 June 1961, passing Dawlish Warren. *M. Pope*

Bottom right:
Once a major railway centre, the importance of Newton Abbot has progressively declined over the past quarter century. Here, with the extensive railway works on the left, 'King' No 6015 *King Richard III* heads east with the up 'Cornish Riviera Limited' on 18 July 1956. The locomotive carries one of the versions of the final headboard style bearing the title 'Limited' rather than 'Express'. *R. C. Riley*

of the motive power depot which stands within the triangular junction, and passes Reading West station before taking a route alongside the Kennet and Avon canal. Major rail-served oil and stone terminals are passed on the right side of the line just west of Theale station, on the site of the Great Western's permanent way depot. The scenery then becomes a pleasant mixture of rural country and 'silicone valley' industrial development as local stations are passed at Aldermaston, Midgham and Thatcham. Between the first two were the water troughs where the steam-hauled 'Cornish Riviera' would have picked up its first replenishment of water since leaving Paddington. At Thatcham the huge paper works is being progressively engulfed by development, which spreads along towards Newbury, whose racecourse, with its own station, lies south of the line.

At Newbury little can now be seen either of the Didcot, Newbury & Southampton line, or the branch to Lambourn. The main line starts to climb as it follows the canal closely through Kintbury and across Hungerford Common, to pass the restored Crofton Pumping station on a curve, to the north of the line. Here, the Cornish beam engines kept water in the upper levels of the canal. At Savernake there is now no station, but the site is marked by earthworks and remains of bridges on both sides of the line where the Cheltenham-Andover line crossed overhead and the Marlborough branch diverged. Here the canal is carried under the station site in a 500yd tunnel from which it emerges, now on the north side of the main line.

Near Pewsey, one of the ancient white horses may be seen carved on a hill to the south of the line, while Pewsey station is now the only original Berks & Hants Extension Railway station left standing. Little can now be seen of Patney & Chirton station, junction for the old line to Devizes, but another white horse is encountered on the approach to Westbury. Here, the non-stop 'Cornish Riviera' bypasses Westbury station by an avoiding line to the south and passes under the Westbury-Salisbury line. In steam days a slip portion was detached here for the Weymouth line.

The sidings around Westbury and Frome, avoided by another short bypass line, are nowadays full of stone hopper wagons which work from the quarries on the former Frome-Radstock and Cheddar valley lines. Beyond the local station at Bruton, the route of the erstwhile Somerset & Dorset line crosses the main line and at Castle Cary the Weymouth line turns away southwards. Somerton Tunnel, the first to be encountered on this route, is passed before Curry Rivell Junction is reached. This was where the line from Yeovil converged from the south. The main line route now turns south-westwards to join the Bristol-Taunton 'Great Way Round' route at Cogload Junction on the approach to Taunton. Here, in steam days, a second section was slipped from the train.

Today's IC125 High Speed Trains no longer need to take advantage of the shorter Berks and Hants route in order to

Above:
Up trains from Plymouth face the formidable climb of Hemerdon bank, 2½ miles at 1 in 42 and a further 7 miles less steep, to the summit at Rattery. Here, 'Western' No D1073 *Western Bulwark* approaches the summit, near the site of Wrangaton station, on 4 June 1971. *J. H. Cooper-Smith*

Left:
The down train is here seen approaching Plymouth station on an unrecorded date. 'Warship' No D817 *Foxhound* carries the final style headboard bearing the 'Express' wording and the fourth and fifth vehicles in the train are one of the ex-GWR kitchen/restaurant pairs liveried in brown and cream to match the BR Mk 1 stock in use on the 'Cornish Riviera' service. *A. A. Sellman*

reduce the journey time. Accordingly the current Sundays Paddington-Penzance service designated as the 'Cornish Riviera' has reverted to the original route via Bristol.

Beyond the station there are engineers' sidings before the site of Norton Fitzwarren is reached. Here the severed connection to the now-preserved Minehead branch can be seen to the right, together with the track bed of the much-lamented picturesque route to Barnstaple. There now follows a steep climb up Wellington bank, to the summit at Whiteball tunnel. It was here, in 1904 that the locomotive *City of Truro* put up its 100mph performance which heralded the dawn of high-speed expresses to the West of England.

After crossing the county border into Devon, the site of Tiverton Junction station is passed and little can now been seen of its branches, eastwards to Hemyock and westwards to Tiverton. This station closed in 1986 on being replaced by the new Tiverton Parkway which serves the M5 motorway, now visible on the left of the line.

From here it is only a few minutes' run to Exeter and as the city is approached the former Southern main line from Plymouth can be seen converging from the right. Rationalisation has reduced the Southern route to a single line branch, and even the familiar landmark of Cowley Bridge Junction signalbox has now gone. The Southern line splits at Yeoford to serve Barnstaple, and formerly divided at Meldon to serve Bude and Padstow, the main route continuing to Plymouth. It is now truncated at Meldon to serve the railway ballast quarry there, and only an infrequent passenger service to Barnstaple now operates. Services to Bude, Padstow and to Plymouth via Okehampton all ceased with the Beeching Report.

Perhaps the most curious railway feature of Exeter was that between Cowley Bridge Junction and Exeter St Davids southern and western trains shared the same tracks but

Left:
The 'Cornish Riviera' had become a very nondescript affair by the time this view of the up train crossing Brunel's Royal Albert Bridge, Saltash, was taken on 5 July 1979. No 47477 has charge of the Mk 2 air-conditioned stock. *B. Morrison*

Below left:
A passenger's eye view from the up 'Cornish Riviera' as it crosses from Cornwall into Devon on a summer day in 1960. *P. Q. Treloar*

Bottom left:
Immaculate new 'Warship' No D805 *Benbow* hustles the up 'Cornish Riviera' through Liskeard station on 23 May 1959. *M. Mensing*

the Plymouth-bound 'Cornish Riviera' and all down Western trains would pass down Southern trains coming in the opposite direction. A glance at a map shows how the two routes crossed in this curious fashion. Exeter St Davids (173 miles from London) is now the first stop for the 'Cornish Riviera'.

Leaving the city the train heads across flat land with the River Exe estuary growing ever wider on the left. There were once water troughs between the site of Exminster station and Starcross, where the locomotive would again replenish its tender. I well recall being in the leading brake van of an express, coupled immediately behind the tender, on this stretch. As we hit the troughs the leading gangway connection proved far from waterproof and in seconds we were paddling in half an inch of water!

Starcross station stands close to the sea shore, and adjacent to it is the large red sandstone engine house which was built to exhaust air from the tubes on Brunel's atmospheric railway. Along the coast through Dawlish Warren, Dawlish and Teignmouth, is perhaps the best known section of the West Country railway. Few South Devon holidaymakers will be unfamiliar with the sight of expresses wending their way along the foot of the cliffs and plunging in and out of the tunnels which abound here.

The next major station is Newton Abbot, some 20 miles from Exeter, where the remaining section of the closed Moretonhampstead branch can be seen converging from the right. Beyond the station, at the site of Aller Junction (the actual junction was removed during resignalling in 1987) the Torbay line to Torquay and Paignton, which leads to the preserved Paignton-Kingswear section, turns away to the left.

On the main line there follows the steep climb to Dainton Tunnel and then the preserved Dart Valley Railway, formerly the branch from Totnes to Ashburton, is seen on the right as Totnes station is approached. There is then another steep climb, up Rattery bank to Marley Tunnel. Several closed station sites are discernible on the next stretch, including Brent, once the junction for the branch to Kingsbridge. Several fine viaducts also feature on the descent of Hemerdon bank towards Ply-

Right:
The up 'Cornish Riviera' is only a few minutes out of Penzance as it crosses Hayle viaduct behind 'Western' No D1058 *Western Nobleman* on 26 July 1975. *B. Morrison*

mouth. Here the remaining short stub of the branch to Launceston converges through goods sidings on the right, while the important Laira Motive Power Depot is seen below the main line to the left.

The 'Cornish Riviera' stops at Plymouth North Road station where the modern 1960s station has obliterated all trace of its predecessor which, for much of its career, was the 'Riviera's' first stop.

Departure from Plymouth (225 miles from Paddington) is soon followed by the entry into Cornwall over the single track of Brunel's magnificent Royal Albert Bridge at Saltash. Though it is nowadays overshadowed by the adjacent road bridge it still offers magnificent views over the Tamar estuary.

Many of the local stations in Cornwall remain open to passengers, but the 'Cornish Riviera' calls only at the principal ones. Since the 'Riviera' implies 'coast' and the main line is very much inland, a number of stops are made to connect with branch line trains to coastal resorts. The first is at Liskeard where the station's hilltop location provides for high viaducts on both sides. Here the train connects for Looe, the branch line turning through almost 360°, leaving the station on the north side and turning to pass under the main line east of Liskeard and continuing to Coombe Junction in the shadow of Moorswater viaduct, west of Liskeard, where the branch trains reverse to reach Looe.

The next stop is amid wooded scenery at Bodmin Parkway, formerly Bodmin Road station, where the abandoned branch to Bodmin is being reactivated by preservationists. The stop at Par, a rural junction in the heart of china clay country provides for the branch connection to Newquay, a *real* 'Riviera' holiday resort. Next is the important town of St Austell, followed by Truro, a fine cathedral city and junction of the branch to Falmouth, whose train also connects with the 'Riviera'. Redruth and Camborne follow, and the countryside starts to take on the 'windswept' look which shows that the sea is now only a few miles away on either side. St Erth, near the head of the Hayle estuary serves only a few surrounding industries but provides the connection for St Ives, just 4½ miles away along a scenic branch line.

Now within sight of the sea, the railway skirts Mounts Bay, with views of St Michaels Mount as it crosses the causeway past Long Rock carriage sidings and the heliport. From here helicopters operate scheduled services to the Scilly Isles. The fine stone-built terminus, close to the seafront at Penzance is nowadays reached a shade under 5hr after leaving Paddington, more than 2hr having been gradually whittled from the original Great Western schedule.

Above:
The 10.40 Penzance-Paddington 'Cornish Riviera', formed by IC125 unit No 253.029 passes the camping coaches at the site of Marazion station on 27 June 1982. Mounts Bay and Cornwall's 'Riviera' coastline are visible above the camping coaches. *B. Morrison*

Below:
BR Standard 'Britannia' 4-6-2 No 70019 *Lightning* brings the down 'Cornish Riviera' into Penzance in October 1951. The ex-GWR stock is in carmine and cream livery. *B. A. Butt*

CHAPTER THREE

The Service in GWR Days

In the early years of the present century, the Great Western Railway's preoccupation with speeding up services to Plymouth was primarily concerned with the lucrative ocean liner traffic. Plymouth was at that time a principal port of call for Trans-Atlantic liners on passage to and from Southampton. Passengers and goods which went by rail between Plymouth and London could do so considerably quicker than by travelling via Southampton. The London & South Western Railway (LSWR) was contracted to carry the passengers on this route, while the Great Western carried the mail. Despite having the less glamorous aspect of the operation, the GWR could expect good publicity value from its efforts to carry the mail ever-faster, and a considerable rivalry had developed. Any speeding up of London-Plymouth services would also be to Cornwall's benefit by shortening the overall journey time to the far west.

The key to reducing journey times lay initially in constructing a more direct route than that via Bristol, which had earned the uncomplimentary nickname 'the Great Way Round'. The Berks & Hants line section was a long straggling branch line from Reading which had been progressively extended through Newbury to terminate at Devizes. The Direct line was to diverge at Patney & Chirton, leaving Devizes on a branch line, and run via Lavington to Westbury, thence to Frome, Witham and Castle Cary with a new section onwards to link up with the old route near Taunton.

Other developments were taking place simultaneously, particularly with regard to motive power, and these would enable faster journey times to the west before the new route was complete. So it was that on 14 July 1903, one of George Jackson Churchward's new 'City' 4-4-0 locomotives, No 3433 *City of Bath*, whisked a Royal train from Paddington to Plymouth (246 miles non-stop via Bristol) at an average speed of 63.4mph. The load was five bogie coaches including the Royal saloon and the journey took 3hr 53½min. On 9 May 1904 a sister locomotive, No 3440 *City of Truro*, as part of the rivalry with the LSWR, took an up ocean mails special from Plymouth to Paddington in 3hr 47min including a reputed maximum of 102mph down Wellington bank in Somerset.

Although these achievements were made in comfort and safety, Edwardian fears of high speed were such that they were not publicised at the time. They did, however,

Below:
An early 20th century view of Penzance station. On the left an 0-6-0ST is performing station pilot duties, while 'Bulldog' No 3428 *River Plym* waits to depart with an up express.
Ian Allan Library

herald the dawn of regular express running to Plymouth with much improved timings and with a prestige train.

The stage was thus set for a major improvement in services to the far west centred around the introduction of a new Paddington-Penzance train which would run non-stop between Paddington and Plymouth and would be named 'The Cornish Riviera Limited'. I have used the title here as written in the Great Western's account of the train's history on its 25th anniversary. The definite article is not normally used within train names, and though there have been changes from time to time, the simple title 'Cornish Riviera' has usually been carried by the train, without either 'Limited' or 'Express'.

The precise reasoning behind the 'Limited' has puzzled me. Consensus suggests that, like the Pullman Car Company, the GWR used the word to indicate that accommodation was limited to the number of seats available on the train (ie standing passengers would not be carried). However, I had always felt that it was more appropriate to the limited stops made by the service. In any event, railwaymen generally referred to it simply as 'The Limited'. At the time of its launch the train was not named and there is no mention of a name in the contemporary report published in *Railway Gazette* in July 1904. Its original title 'The Riviera Express' was the result of a competition in the 1904 *Railway Magazine* which attracted 1,286 entries, the winning name being chosen by Sir James Inglis, General Manager of the GWR.

The launch took place on 1 July 1904, the down train leaving Paddington at 10.10am while the up working left Penzance at 10.00am. No regular, daily,

Top right:
Each new express passenger locomotive class quickly found employment on the 'Cornish Riviera' and here the down train is seen on the Dawlish seafront behind 4-6-0 No 100. The date is 1904, before this section had been double-tracked, and the train is the clerestory-roofed original stock with the 'Dreadnought' dining car.
LGRP/Courtesy David & Charles (21407)

Above right:
Churchward's 'Star' 4-6-0s gave way to 'Castles' in the mid-1920s and here a down Sunday working is seen in Twyford cutting behind No 5003 *Lulworth Castle*. *Real Photographs (705)*

Right:
At this time the 'Cornish Riviera' had become a heavy train of 14 vehicles leaving Paddington and it quickly became a routine duty for 'Kings'. Here, the second part of the down train, made up of vehicles from Collett bow-ended stock, gets into its stride on the Berks & Hants line with No 6007 *King William III* in charge. *Real Photographs (717)*

The inaugural 'Cornish Riviera' of 1 July 1904 passes Old Oak Common with de Glehn compound 4-4-2 No 102 *La France* at the head of six coaches including a 'Dreadnought' dining car. Painted by George Heiron from an original photograph in the Locomotive Publishing Co collection.

non-stop runs of such length had been attempted before, and the train of six coaches including a dining car was a substantial load for a 4-4-0 over such a route.

The time allowed for the down journey was 4hr 25min and included a single stretch in excess of 80 miles to be covered at an average speed of more than 60mph. On the day before the service was launched a test run was made in the down direction using 4-4-0 No 3433 *City of Bath* and the six coaches which would form the first up train. The train reached Plymouth ½min early and, after changing locomotives, Penzance was reached 13min early at 4.57pm.

The inaugural down working was headed by the French-built de Glehn 'Compound' 4-4-2 No 102 *La France*, as far as Plymouth, while the up train left Penzance behind a 'City' 4-4-0. The formation comprised clerestory-roofed 52ft corridor coaches, brake third, third, first, dining car (70ft 'Dreadnought' type), second, brake third, with a loaded weight of 189 tons. Seating capacity was for 200 passengers.

On the down run, 59.6mph was averaged from London to Exeter, including 100 miles at 64.6mph average and a maximum speed of 75mph. The up train achieved an average of 62.1mph including no less than 200 miles at an average of 61mph and a maximum of 81mph.

Such was the success of the new train that within a year new rolling stock was under construction. The trains were still formed of six vehicles, but all were now of the elliptical-roofed 'Dreadnought' pattern. The nickname, taken from the battleships of the day, referred to the massive nature of these coaches. At 9ft 6in wide they were a full 1ft wider than their predecessors, and all were around 70ft long. The formation was: brake third, third, first/third composite, dining car, first/third composite, brake third.

In the dining car, the first and third class saloons were separated by the central kitchen, while in the corridor third and composites there was a novel arrangement of the corridor which switched from one side of the vehicle to the other mid-way along its length. This was said to improve weight distribution and provide for better viewing of the passing scenery.

There was also a novel method of seat reservation. Each seat was numbered and station masters at each of the train's stops were provided with a seating diagram. For the charge of 1s 0d (5p) the passenger would be supplied with a ticket giving his reserved seat number. This practice, which came to be known as seat regulation, would eventually become compulsory on most expresses to the West Country during the holiday season. It provided a means of assessing in advance the need for extra accommodation or the running of relief services.

The completion of the shortened route via the Berks & Hants line and Castle Cary, with its new water troughs provided at Aldermaston and between Westbury and Frome, enabled the route to be shortened by just under 20 miles and the journey time cut to 4hr 7min (Paddington-Plymouth) and 6hr 35min to Penzance. On the down train, running by the new route, coaches were slipped at Taunton to serve Minehead, and Ilfracombe (via Barnstaple). Departure time from Paddington was altered to 10.30am, a time which was to become synonymous with the 'Cornish Riviera' throughout the Great Western period, and, until recently, with little change during the BR period.

There followed a 'golden age' during which the nature of the 'Cornish Riviera' changed little. The train was to become an early candidate for rostering of the newest and best in motive power and the pattern was established during this period when Churchward's new four-cylinder 'Star' class 4-6-0s took over the duty. The appearance of the train itself changed for a spell when the GWR forsook its chocolate and cream coach livery in favour of an all-over dark lake colour.

The stability and confidence which had been built up during the Victorian era and had reached its zenith in the Edwardian England into which the 'Cornish Riviera' was born, was drawing to a close. Two events would bring down the curtain on an era, and people would never again feel quite the same. On the night of 14/15 April 1912, the epitome of human engineering skill and the ultimate statement of grandeur and confidence, the SS *Titanic*, struck an iceberg whilst on her maiden voyage to New York. *Titanic* sank in 2½hr with the loss of 1,500 lives. It was to herald the closing of an era of grace and confidence in travel.

Within two years of this tragedy Europe was plunged into the 'Great War' — a title which conjures up, more than any other, the nature of those four years of bloody carnage. Inevitably, the railways of Britain were brought under government control. Towards the end of 1916, the authorities were calling on the railway companies to supply vast quantities of track and rolling stock to support the troops bogged down in the trenches in France. Locally available rail systems were vastly over-stretched. The railways responded positively to the call, but pointed out that their own systems were also overtaxed by the war effort. Materials and equipment could only be made available by a package of measures including passenger service reductions, reductions in speed of operations, and even by the closure of some minor lines.

So the needs of war saw the 'Cornish Riviera' progressively reduced from its prestige nature, slowed down and with additional stops introduced when necessary. Arrears of maintenance took their toll even on the Great Western's finest. Although the 'Limited' continued to run throughout the war, economies such as the Sunday closing of branch lines (including St Ives), made access to parts of the West Country that much more difficult. Indeed, one line, the independent Bideford, Westward Ho! & Appledore Railway, was closed completely and its components requisitioned for wartime use elsewhere, never to reopen.

Having lopped another 5min off the schedule in 1914, the war saw the Paddington-Penzance time increased by 1¼hr resulting from additional stops at Westbury, Taunton, Exeter, Newton Abbot and additional Cornish stations. The return to normal after the war, commenced on 7 July 1919 when non-stop running to Plymouth was restored, although at a slower timing (4¼hr) than previously. Penzance was reached in a further 3hr.

The following year saw the reintroduction of the Westbury slip from the down train, and for the winter timetable, starting 3 October 1921, all three slips (Westbury, Taunton, Exeter) were provided and the pre-war timings resumed.

Throughout this period the 'Star' 4-6-0s had almost exclusive charge of the 'Cornish Riviera', but in the early 1920s under the new Chief Mechanical Engineer, C. B. Collett, further developments in motive power took place. The successor to the 'Star' was introduced in 1923 with No 4073 *Caerphilly Castle*. In the following year the first members of the 'Castle' class took over the 'Cornish Riviera'. So successful were they, that new batches with detail variations, but to the same basic design, would continue to be built until 1950. The 'Castle' 4-6-0s were to have charge of the Paddington-Plymouth section of the 'Limited' for only a couple of years however, for they were to be displaced by a larger and heavier development, the 'King' 4-6-0. 'Castles' would continue to stand in for 'Kings' throughout their career, however, and since the 'Kings' were not permitted over the Saltash bridge, 'Castles' worked the train through Cornwall until the advent of the 'Counties' and BR Standard 4-6-2s.

The Great Western's boastful publicity for the new 'Castle' class which accompanied the locomotive exhibited at the Empire Exhibition, led to an exchange with the London & North Eastern Railway in 1925. 'Castle' No 4079 *Pendennis Castle* was set to work on the East Coast main line, while the Gresley 4-6-2 No 4474 *Victor Wild* went west for trials on the 'Cornish Riviera'. The story of this exchange has been well documented elsewhere. Suffice to say here that the Great Western perpetuated and developed the 'Castle' design, while Gresley returned to the drawing board to incorporate principles of the GWR design into his future products.

During the 1920s the Great Western's publicity department really got into its stride and began the practice that we would now call 'merchandising.' Apart from promoting the Company's services, a whole range of products began to be offered, including books and jigsaws to while away the time on the journey. Inevitably, the company's prestige train was an ideal subject for a book and the *The 10.30 Limited* was a chance to trumpet the company's achievements in numerous areas, as well as telling the story of the 'Cornish Riviera' and its route.

The first of the 'King' class 4-6-0s appeared in 1927 and once these locomotives had taken over the 'Cornish Riviera' between Paddington and Plymouth, the journey time was reduced to 4hr

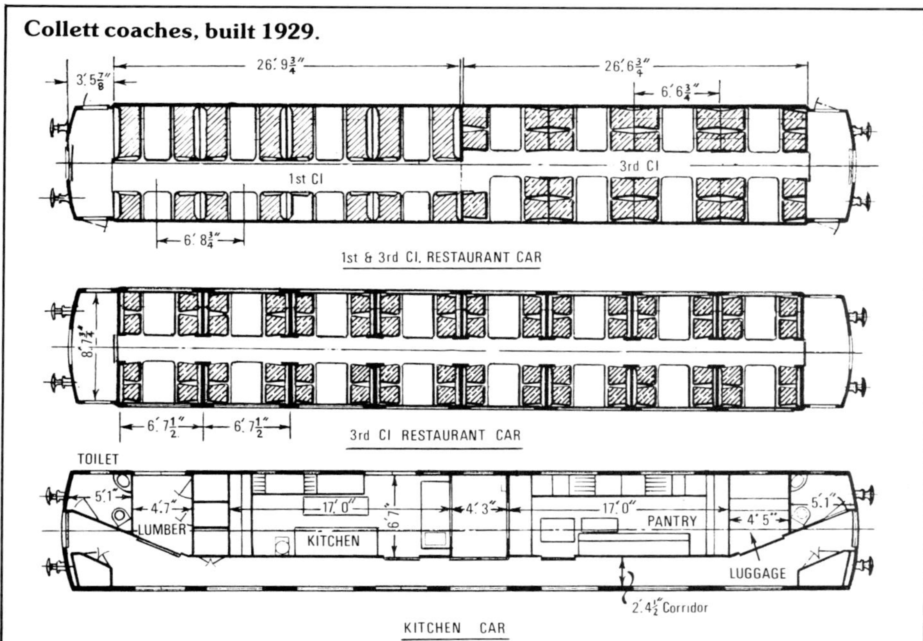

Collett coaches, built 1929.

Table 1: Composition of the 'Cornish Riviera' 1929

No of Compartments	*No of Passengers*		*Tare Weight TC*		
Brake third (2)	16		32	10	
Third (8)	64		34	3	
Third (8)	64		34	3	
Third dining saloon	64		32	11	
Kitchen car	—		42	13	Penzance section
First and third dining saloon	24 1st;	31 3rd	32	17	
First (4) and third composite (3)	24 1st;	24 3rd	34	3	
Brake third (2)	16		32	10	
First (2) and third brake composite (4)	12 1st;	32 3rd	34	5	Through coaches to St Ives
First (2) and third brake composite (4)	12 1st;	32 3rd	34	5	Through coaches to Falmouth
First (2) and third brake composite (4)	12 1st;	32 3rd	34	5	Detached at Plymouth
Double-ended (2) slip (4)	12 1st;	32 3rd	36	6	Slipped at Westbury
First (2) and third brake composite (4)	12 1st;	32 3rd	34	5	for Weymouth

and the load increased again. By now the peak summer loadings were becoming such that a single 'Cornish Riviera' was insufficient and up to three relief trains might be operated.

The train's 25th anniversary was marked in 1929 with the introduction of new rolling stock. At this time it was estimated that over 3 million passengers had used the train and that 5 million miles had been run by the service. Publicity at the time recalled that it had sustained its status as the world's longest non-stop run until two years previously, and that it was the only train to convey three slip portions. Such had been the success of the latter, that they were now only operated during the winter. Summer services conveyed only the Westbury slip for Weymouth, the traffic on the other sections being such as to warrant complete separate trains.

The new coaches were 9ft 6in over panels, in order to provide greater internal width and improved comfort. The extreme width was accompanied by a reduction in overall length to avoid excessive end overhang and with a length of c60ft it was still necessary to recess the end doors and handles to bring them within the loading gauge. Nevertheless, these Collett 'bow-enders' were handsome steel-panelled vehicles with steam heating, electric light and Vita glass. The latter was said to be extremely healthy as it admitted all the sun's ultra violet rays. It was also fitted almost flush with the vehicle's external panelling giving an improved appearance.

Total accommodation was for 428 passengers, and there was seating in the restaurant cars for 24 first class and 95 third class passengers. No more than two sittings were required in order to serve the entire complement of passengers.

The interiors were finished with 'Empire timbers', while extensive use of stainless steel was made in the kitchens. The latter were arranged to be unusually roomy and were provided with a stewards' section so that waiters could obtain their supplies without blocking the corridors. Plate warmers (capacity 400 plates) and refrigerators were fitted, and the vehicles were equipped with real wine cellars fitted into the floor. Slip coaches to match the new stock were double-ended with a slip guard's compartment at either end to obviate the need for turning at the end of each journey. The complete composition of the summer train was as shown in the accompanying table.

In the early 1930s there followed further line improvements with the opening of the flying junction at Cogload and quadrupling of track thence through a rebuilt Taunton station to Norton Fitzwarren. Bypassing lines or 'cut-offs' were then built to enable non-stop trains to avoid Westbury and Frome.

The next major event was the GWR Centenary in 1935 which marked the 100th anniversary of the forming of the company rather than the more usual anniversary of the opening. The event was marked with more new coaching stock to the maximum available dimensions and equipped to the most luxurious standard. Trains of this 'Centenary' stock were allocated to the 'Cornish Riviera' for the summer 1935 service.

The 10-coach formation was made up as follows:

Brake composite	(36 seats)
Brake composite	(36 seats)
Third	(56 seats)
Brake third	(16 seats)
Composite	(48 seats)
Kitchen first	(24 seats)
Third diner	(64 seats)
Third	(56 seats)
Third	(56 seats)
Brake third	(16 seats)

A large number of brake vehicles was included for the various through portions, but overall there was a slight reduction in accomodation at 324 third class and 84 first. Once slip portions were added to the train, its handsome uniformity would have been sacrificed as there were no matching slip coaches. The reduction in accommodation was alleviated by operating the train with the new stock as the 'Cornish Riviera Limited', which departed from Paddington at 10.30am and running a second service, the 'Cornishman' with conventional stock 5min later. The new 'Limited' was booked non-stop to Truro on weekdays and to St Erth on Saturdays.

By the outbreak of World War 2 the credit for the longest non-stop run had been snatched by the LMS and LNER with their non-stop services from London to Scotland. The initial impact of the war was to curtail all such extravagances, but in the summer of 1939 the Great Western's reinstatement of the 'Cornish Riviera' via the shorter route with Exeter as first stop regained the distinction. As wartime economies and restrictions began to bite, the 'Limited' was combined with the 'Torbay Express' and decelerated with additional stops. By 1941 the two trains were separated again, but further slowed. In 1943 the GWR revealed its plans for the painting of coaches in a plain 'utility' brown colour, but one or two prestige trains, including the 'Cornish Riviera' would be spared this indignity.

After the war the GWR, like the other railway companies, began the process of reconstruction. New coaches built to modern standards and designed by the new Chief Mechanical Engineer, F. W. Hawksworth, soon emerged from Swindon works. By May 1946 it was possible to restore 4½hr timings to Plymouth and 6hr 55min through to Penzance.

On March 20 1947 the 'Cornish Riviera' was the subject of a question in the House of Commons Fuel shortages had led to the service being withdrawn on Government instructions. The MP for St Ives asked how much fuel would be saved by this measure

Above:
Hawksworth 'County' 4-6-0 No 1007 *County of Brecknock* heads a colourful mixture of Mk 1 coaching stock forming the down 'Cornish Riviera' through Saltash in August 1959.
T. B. Owen/Colour-Rail No BRW602

Below:
Travel-stained 'Manor' 4-6-0 No 7806 *Cockington Manor* leads 'Castle' No 7006 *Lydford Castle* off Forder Viaduct with the up 'Cornish Riviera' in July 1959.
P. W. Gray/Colour-Rail No BRW620

Below:
One of the final style headboards for the 'Cornish Riviera Express' was displayed at Didcot railway centre during 1987 as part of the exhibition marking the diamond jubilee of 'King' No 6000 *King George V*. *Author*

Bottom:
One of the early NBL 'Warship' diesel-hydraulics, No D602 *Bulldog* heads the up 'Cornish Riviera' across Largin Viaduct.
B. J. Swain/Colour-Rail No DE 590

1935 'Centenary' coaching stock.

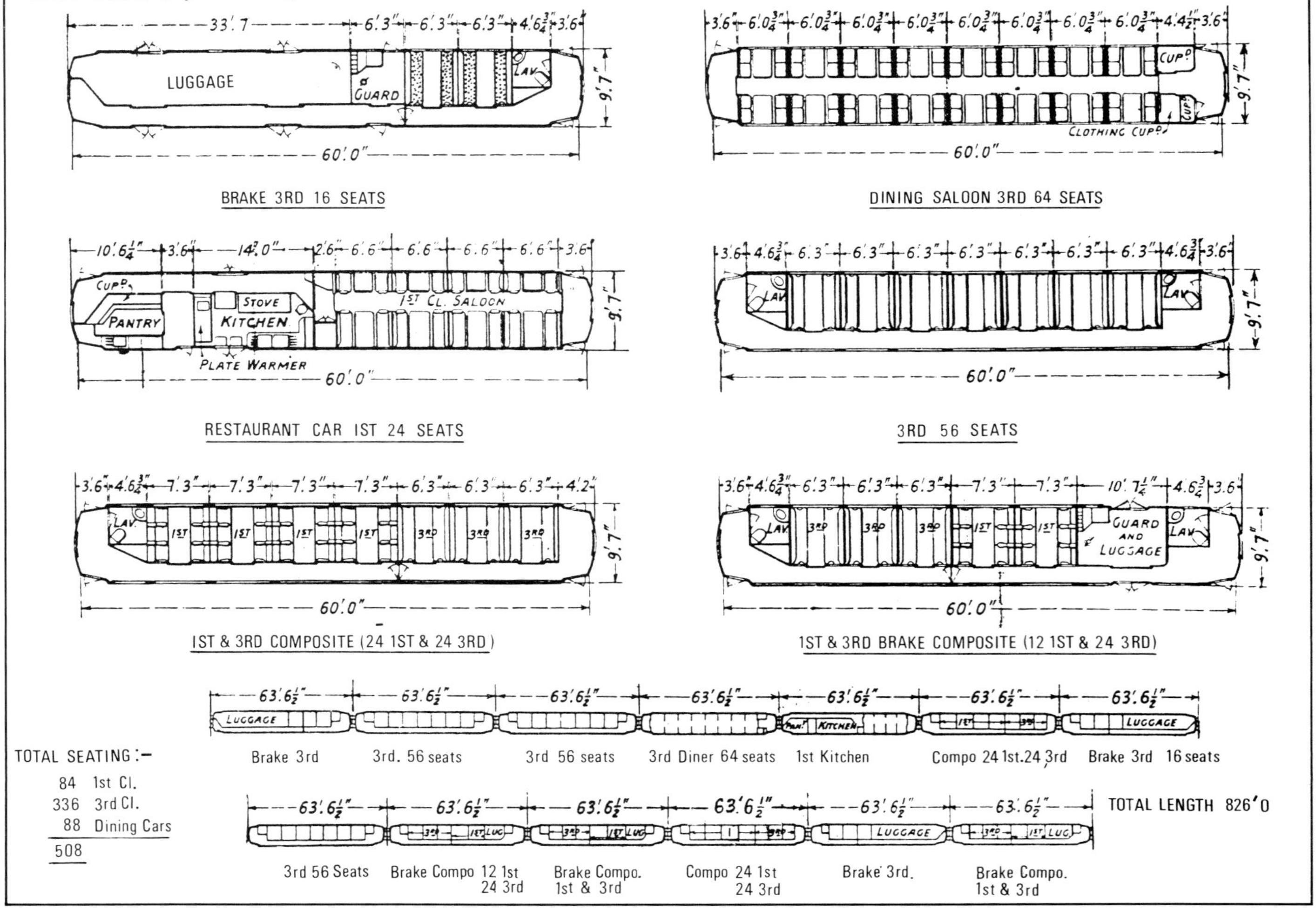

LUGGAGE
GUARD
LAV

BRAKE 3RD 16 SEATS

CLOTHING CUPD.

DINING SALOON 3RD 64 SEATS

PANTRY
STOVE
KITCHEN
PLATE WARMER
1ST CL. SALOON

RESTAURANT CAR 1ST 24 SEATS

3RD 56 SEATS

1ST & 3RD COMPOSITE (24 1ST & 24 3RD)

GUARD AND LUGGAGE

1ST & 3RD BRAKE COMPOSITE (12 1ST & 24 3RD)

Brake 3rd | 3rd. 56 seats | 3rd 56 seats | 3rd Diner 64 seats | 1st Kitchen | Compo 24 1st.24 3rd | Brake 3rd 16 seats

3rd 56 Seats | Brake Compo 12 1st 24 3rd | Brake Compo. 1st & 3rd | Compo 24 1st 24 3rd | Brake 3rd. | Brake Compo. 1st & 3rd

TOTAL LENGTH 826'0

TOTAL SEATING :-

84 1st Cl.
336 3rd Cl.
88 Dining Cars
508

and was advised that some 110 tons per week was being saved. However, 16 June 1947 saw the train restored for the duration of the summer timetable, albeit with an 11am departure from Paddington and stops at Taunton and Exeter.

Thus the 'Cornish Riviera' saw out the final days of the Great Western Railway. Like many features of the company which founded it, the service was to rise to new and greater heights during the years which followed Nationalisation in 1948.

Right:
'Castle' class 4-6-0 No 5079 *Lysander* passes Marazion with the 'Cornish Riviera Express' on 25 August 1947.
A. C. Cawston

Reproduced from *Locomotive Magazine*
14 January 1928

ON THE FOOTPLATE OF THE CORNISH RIVIERA EXPRESS.

By DOUGLAS SEATON.

OWING to the courtesy of Mr. C. B. Collett, C.B.E., Chief Mechanical Engineer of the Great Western Ry., I had the privilege of travelling from London to Plymouth on the footplate of No. 6005 *King George II* hauling the Cornish Riviera Express.

The formation of the train was as follows:—two 70 ft. coaches to be slipped at Westbury for the Weymouth line; a 70 ft. for Minehead and a 60 ft. for Ilfracombe, to be slipped at Taunton; a 70 ft. and a 60 ft. for Exeter and a 70 ft. for the Kingsbridge line, to be slipped at Exeter. The Cornish part of the train comprised 70 ft. coaches for Newquay, Falmouth and St. Ives, and the through portion to Penzance was made up of a four coach set including restaurant car. The tare loads were therefore:—

Paddington-Westbury	489 tons
Westbury-Taunton	401 ,,
Taunton-Exeter	357 ,,
Exeter-Plymouth	256 ,,

On the stroke of 10-30 a.m., the departure time of the train, we drew away from No. 1 platform and accelerated in the manner of an electric train, touching the mile a minute rate before Hanwell.

As we left, Driver Wimhurst beckoned me to sit on the tip-up seat immediately behind where he stood. Although these seats can hardly be compared to a well-padded arm-chair, they afford an excellent view point for watching the handling of the engine, and also for checking speed by the quarter mile posts along the line. One can only suppose that they are provided for the use of enginemen when waiting for their trains. Certainly sitting down played no part in the programme of Driver Wimhurst or his fireman.

Adverse signals at Maidenhead and Reading cost us three minutes, and a further unfortunate check at Newbury Racecourse was not the most propitious of starts for the long climb to Savernake. Reference to the two tables will give some idea of the tremendous power of the engine. Over the thirteen miles from Newbury to Bedwyn with gradients steepening from 1 in 600 to 1 in 400 with short stretches at 1 in 169, the average speed was 63·8 m.p.h. From Bedwyn to Savernake the bank stiffens to 1 in 140 until the summit is crossed 415 ft. above Paddington. Over this last section speed was 49·2 m.p.h.

A glance at the cut-off and regulator table will show that 17 per cent. cut-off with 18 per cent. for the last ¾-mile before the top, was sufficient to produce this truly remarkable performance with a gross load well in excess of 500 tons. I expected to be surprised, but this was something in the nature of an apocalypse!

Down the chalky Wiltshire slopes we dashed, touching 80 m.p.h. at Pewsey and onwards through Patney till a slight application of the brakes brought us down to 75 m.p.h. at Lavington.

At Westbury we lost the tip of our tail and breasted the rising gradients to Frome and Witham with but little effort on the part of the engine. The famous mile post 122¾ marking the crest of Witham bank had come and gone almost before one realised that another steep hill had been surmounted.

Down Bruton bank high speed was again reached and maintained to the P.W. relaying check east of Somerton. As we picked up we entered a tunnel and in spite of the fact that the huge machine was accelerating hard with a heavy train there was little or no reverberation from the brick arch a foot or so above the funnel, which silence spells efficiency in large letters.

Taunton was passed 1½ minutes behind time owing to the various delays which we had suffered. However, relieved of a further two coaches we made a fast climb up Whiteball and sped down the flooded valley of the Exe to slip three coaches at Exeter thirty seconds behind scheduled time. Running carefully over the winding coastal section behind Starcross and Teignmouth we soon sighted the rebuilt station at Newton Abbot, and ahead lay what might literally be termed the *Pièce de resistance* of the journey, for the gradients between Newton Abbot and Plymouth are the steepest over which any express service of this nature is operated in any part of the world, but such is the power of *King George II* that not once did he give any indication of being hard pressed and certainly the idea of pilot assistance never entered his head. Heavy rain clouds drifting off Dartmoor caused the spectacle windows to become somewhat obscured, and the driver found invaluable the motor-car type of windscreen wiper with which the latest locomotives are fitted.

Table 2: 'Cornish Riviera' timings 21/11/27

Record of running of 10.30am passenger train — Paddington to Plymouth North Road — 21 November, 1927

Stations	*Booked Times Arr Dep*	*Actual Times Arr Dep*	*Load tons*	*Distance miles chains*	*Speed mph*	*Remarks*
Paddington	10-30	10-30	489			
Southall	10-41	10-42		9.6	45.4	
Slough	10-50	10-51		9.30	62.5	
Farnham Road						2min signal check
Maidenhead						1min signal check
Reading	11-7	11-10		17.42	55.6	
Newbury Racecourse						
Newbury	11-25½	11.28½		17.9	55.5	1min signal check
Bedwyn	11-38½	11-41		13.26	63.8	
Savernake	11-42½	11-45½		3.55	49.2	
Westbury	12-6	12-7	401	25.37	71.0	Slip
Castle Cary	12-28	12-29		19.63	54.0	
Somerton	12-50	12-52		22.42	58.7	2min relaying check
Cogload Junction Taunton	12-54½	12-56	357	5.3	75.6	Slip
Whiteball		1.7				
Exeter	1-24½	1-25	256	30.60	63.6	Slip
Newton Abbot	1-48½	1-48		20.18	52.8	
Dainton	1-54½	1-53½		3.70	43.4	
Ashburton Junction	2-0	1-59		4.48	50.2	
Brent	2-9½	2-9		7.6	42.5	
Hemerdon	2-21	2-20½		9.46	50.1	
Plymouth North Road	2-30	2-29		6.56	47.5	

State of weather — small rain. Coal — good. Engine steamed well all the way.

Inspector — H. J. Robinson

Below:
'King' No 6005 *King George II* which worked the trip described here, is seen as it would have appeared in the time. *LPC/Ian Allan Library*

50 007

Class 50 No 50007 *Hercules* is reflected in the still waters of the Kennet & Avon canal as it heads the down 'Cornish Riviera', formed of Mk2 air-conditioned stock, past Crofton on 29 May 1978. *D. Moulden*

A rapid descent at Hemerdon bank enabled us to reach Plymouth one minute ahead of time. 226 miles over a difficult road with a heavy train in under four hours; and this is to the Great Western Ry. an ordinary everyday performance.

The figures show that 6,500 gallons of water were picked up from the four troughs *en route*. Adding the 4,000 gallons in the tender at Paddington and subtracting the 2,200 gallons remaining at Plymouth, an evaporation figure of 8,300 gallons is arrived at. The exhaust injector alone was used throughout. Coal consumption was approximately 4¼ tons.

A word of praise for the crew of *King George II* is certainly well merited. Mr. H. J. Robinson, Locomotive Inspector, rode on the engine, and it is to his kindness that I am indebted for the two tables. His connection with the Great Western Ry. dates from 1882. Quiet and unassuming in manner, the charm of his personality soon becomes apparent, and an acquaintanceship of an hour or two makes clear the reason of the success which he has achieved in his calling.

Driver W. Wimhurst, of Old Oak Running Shed, can also lay claim to long service with the Company, having been in its employment since 1893. During the four hours' journey he did not relax his attention for one moment. Needless to say he has an intimate knowledge of the road, and the manner in which he handled his charge was masterly.

The responsibility of maintaining steam was entrusted to Fireman W. Howkins. So deft was he in his labours that the needle on the steam gauge might have been fixed on the red line denoting correct working pressure. Only once did the pressure fall back to 240 lb. per sq. in., and that was on the easy section between Starcross and Newton Abbot, where the maintenance of full pressure would only have entailed waste of coal. By the time we faced Dainton the needle was well up to 250 lb. per sq. in., and not even the long and trying Rattery bank could pull it back.

When I descended from the footplate and regretfully became an ordinary passenger on the return journey, the impression which remained was that of a super-efficient machine most ably handled.

Hearty congratulations to Mr. Collett and his staff.

Engine 6005 — Cut-off and regulator

Stations	*Regulator*	*Cut-off*	*Load Tons*	*Water Arr Gallons*	*Dep*	*Remarks*
Paddington	¾	70-45	489		4,000	Left 10.30am
O. O. Common E.		17				
Slough East	Drifting	45				
Farnham Road	Full	20				Signal check
Taplow		17				
Maidenhead E.	Drifting	45				Signal check
Maidenhead Station	Full	20-17				
Kennet Bridge	Drifting	45				Reduction through Reading
Reading W. Main	¾	20				
Southcote Junction	Full	17				
Aldermaston	½	17		2,200	3,700	Reduction
Midgham	¼	17				Reduction brakes applied
Midgham Up distant	Full	17				
Newbury Race Course	Drifting	45				Signal check
Newbury East	Full	17				
Grafton Curve		18				
Burbage		15				
Pewsey	½	15				
Patney	¼	15				
Lavington	½	15				
Westbury — North	Drifting	45				Reduction
Westbury — South	¾	20	401	1,700	3,500	Slip
Fairwood	Full	17				
Frome North East	Drifting	45				Reduction Frome
Frome South East	Full	20				
Woodlands		17				
Brewham	¼	17				Brakes applied down incline
124 mile post	Drifting	45				Relaying
C. Cary						Brakes applied
Somerton	Full	20				
L. Sutton Dist.	¾	17				
L. Sutton Station	½	17				
Cogload Junction	Full	17		2,000	3,700	Creech Troughs
Taunton			3			
Wellington		18				
Beam Bridge		19				
Burlescombe	¾	17				
Sampford	¼	17				
Cowley Bridge	Drifting	45				
Exeter	½	15	256			Slip. Brakes used through
Exminster Troughs				2,300	3,800	station
Powderham Park	¼	15				Brakes applied at curves,
Old Quay	¼	15				Powderham to Teignmouth
Hackney	Drifting	45				
N. Abbot West	¾	17				Brakes applied through
Aller	Full	17				station
Stoneycombe Dist.		20				
Stoneycombe	25					
Dainton		17				Brakes applied at curves.
Totnes	Full	17				Dainton to Totnes
Advance signal	Full	17				
Up incline		20				
Up incline		25				
Tigley	30					
Tigley West	25					
Rattery	½	20				
Brent	½	17				Brakes applied round curves
Brent Station	½	17				
Wrangaton	Full	17				Brent to Hemerdon
Ivybridge	Full	17				
Mannamead	Drifting	45		2,200		Plymouth arrive 2.29pm

CHAPTER FOUR

The Service in BR Days

The newly Nationalised railway system was quick to establish its identity on the public 'face' of the railway system and prestige train services received early attention. The green locomotives and 'chocolate and cream' coaches of the Great Western Railway quickly gave way to a new look 'Cornish Riviera'. The 'Kings', as express passenger locomotives in the highest power category, received blue livery lined in black and white, and were in fact the only class where all the locomotives received this livery. Coaching stock was repainted into carmine and cream ('blood and custard') livery. So, the 'Cornish Riviera' took on a more colourful, if less grand, appearance.

The train was also distinguished by a locomotive headboard. This was the first occasion that the 'Cornish Riviera' had carried such a device. The GWR seldom used headboards — the 'Cheltenham Flier' had carried one proclaiming it as the World's fastest train, but this was an ugly rectangular object which did nothing for the good appearance of the train. The BR boards were of a standardised type used on the principal expresses of all regions except the Southern (the latter used a design more suited to the angular styling of its 'air-smoothed' Pacifics). Bearing the words 'Cornish Riviera' in Gill Sans capitals, the headboards were cast in alloy and painted black with polished letters and border. The use of these headboards was one of the simplest and most effective promotional ideas to come from the new organisation.

So, despite the oft-quoted impression that GWR traditions and attitudes were entrenched on the Western Region (WR), the region's prestige trains very quickly received the BR standardised appearance. Thus they were to remain for several years until a relaxation of some areas of influence led to a sudden reversion to the old style.

In 1951 drainage work on the West of England line led to extensive diversions. The 'Cornish Riviera' and other expresses ran via Swindon and Trowbridge to Westbury, but the section from Thingley Junction to Westbury was barred to 'Kings', so the weekday service became a 'Castle' turn with consequent increases in the overall timing. Sunday services ran via the 'Great Way Round' through Bath and Bristol but were consequently able to have 'King' haulage throughout.

From 30 June 1952, the start of that year's summer timetable, the service was accelerated and the 4hr Plymouth timing restored. There followed a fine period in the history of the 'Cornish Riviera' with the train looking its best, complete with headboard, locomotives gradually being returned to the new standard green livery (modelled on the old GWR style), and with new Mk 1 coaching stock entering traffic. With 'Kings' on the Paddington-Plymouth section, the 'CRE' was often being worked in Cornwall by the new BR Standard 'Britannia' Pacifics.

Summer 1955 saw extensive tests being performed on the Western Region with a view to establishing the performance requirements and capabilities of motive power. The tests centred around the 'Kings' and No 6013 *King Henry VIII* ran a number of in-service trials working the 'Cornish

Below:
Postwar, and post-nationalisation the 'Cornish Riviera' took on a very different look although all the equipment was still pure GWR. 'King' No 6027 *King Richard I* sports BR blue livery lined in black and white and heads the 1946 coaching stock wearing carmine and cream BR livery.
M. W. Earley

Top:
Looking every inch a worthy successor to the Great Western, green-liveried 'Warship' No D601 *Ark Royal*, complete with headboard, leads its pristine chocolate and cream Mk 1 stock along the seafront at Dawlish Warren, forming the down 'Cornish Riviera Express'. The dieselised 'Riviera' was only four months old in June 1958. *T. B. Owen/Colour-Rail No DE772*

Above:
Swindon-built 'Warship' No D801 *Vanguard* whisks the down 'Cornish Riviera' past Twyford on a frosty January morning in 1959. *T. B. Owen/Colour-Rail No DE769*

Above:
The early 'Warships' were equipped to carry the steam-era reporting numbers, as displayed here by the Swindon-built prototype, No D800 *Sir Brian Robertson*, approaching the summit between Truro and Chacewater, with the down 'Cornish Riviera Express' on 16 May 1959. *M. Mensing*

Below:
The last locomotive-hauled up 'Cornish Riviera', suitably adorned, pauses at Bradford Junction for the single line token. The train, headed by Class 50, No 50009 *Conqueror*, was diverted via Swindon due to Westbury area resignalling work. The date was 11 May 1980. *D. Moulden*

Top right:
'King' No 6022 *King Edward III* had recently been fitted with improved superheating when caught by the camera, with unmarked tender, heading the down 'Cornish Riviera' near Reading West. Also new was the cast headboard which was to distinguish the train for the first 15 years of the BR era, in various forms. *M. W. Earley*

Centre right:
Sadly, the headboard was not always carried and on 5 July 1951 a rake of assorted ex-GWR stock added to the nondescript appearance of the train as it passed Twyford behind No 6003 *King George IV*. *B. Morrison*

Below:
On 18 April 1952 the down 'Cornish Riviera' arrives at St Erth behind new 'Britannia' Pacific No 70019 *Lightning*, sporting the headboard and with coach roofboards altered to their new position below the gutters. The Pacific will probably have taken over from a 'King' at Plymouth. *B. A. Butt*

Left:
As 'Kings' were not permitted to cross the Saltash bridge, a change of engine was required at Plymouth. On 25 June 1955 a resplendent 'Castle' No 5069 *Isambard Kingdom Brunel* has charge of the carmine and cream Hawksworth stock here seen between Lostwithiel and Bodmin Road. *R. E. Vincent*

Riviera' with the dynamometer car in the formation to record all the technical data of power output, fuel consumption etc. Some fine performances were put up with the full summer load and early arrivals against the four hour timing to Plymouth.

For the third time in its career, the 'Cornish Riviera' was to be treated to 'foreign' motive power as part of an exchange trial. This had previously happened with the Gresley Pacific in 1925 and with an LMS 'Coronation' 4-6-2 in the 1948 exchanges. For comparison with the 'King' a 'Coronation' was again selected as being the most powerful type available. The London Midland Region (LMR), thoughtfully selected No 46237 *City of Bristol*, the only one of its class bearing a name with Western connections.

Unlike the 1948 trials, in which economy had been the order of the day and the locomotive had been operated by an LMR crew, the 1955 trials had timekeeping on the tightest schedules as their priority, and *City of Bristol* was handled by a Western crew. The train comprised its usual winter formation of nine coaches for Penzance, two to detach at Plymouth and two slipped at Westbury for Weymouth, with the dynamometer car at the front of the formation, giving 14 vehicles in all with a weight around 485 tons.

The first of the down runs took place in pouring rain on a chilly day in May and was fully described by C. J. Allen in the July 1955 issue of *Trains Illustrated*. Suffice to

Above:
At an unrecorded location on the Berks & Hants line a 'King' heads the new look 'Cornish Riviera Limited' with revised headboard and Mk 1 coaches in brown and cream livery. The fifth and sixth vehicles are ex-GWR kitchen/restaurant cars. *Real Photographs*

Right:
The year 1958 brought the change to diesel-hydraulic traction and on 26 July No D601 *Ark Royal*, of the North British 2,000hp 'Warships' is seen heading the 'Cornish Riviera Express' (with steam-era headboard) over Angarrack Viaduct between Hayle and Gwinear Road. *P. Q. Treloar*

The 'Cornish Riviera Limited' at its zenith. In 1935 the Great Western Railway marked its centenary with the construction of new, luxury coaching stock for its prestige services. The 'Centenary' stock forming the 'Limited' is seen headed by a 'King' at Bishopsteignton, in this painting by George Heiron, based on an official GWR photograph.

Left:
The 'Cornish Riviera Express' continues to look smart with diesel traction, and on 2 October 1958 the first of the lighter, more powerful B-B 'Warships', No D800 *Sir Brian Robertson* heads the down train away from St Erth. The non-matching ex-GWR restaurant cars are still in the formation. *B. A. Butt*

Below left:
A year later, use of the headboard was in decline. The same locomotive accelerates the up 'Cornish Riviera' along the causeway out of Penzance, on 23 September 1959. *P. Q. Treloar*

Bottom left:
The 'Cornish Riviera' surely never looked finer than with a green locomotive, steam or diesel, at the head of chocolate and cream stock. The BR Mk 1 coaches looked smart in this livery, but NBL 'Warship' No D601 *Ark Royal* is in need of a clean and a headboard as it heads the down train out of Newton Abbot on 20 February 1960. *W. L. Underhay*

say here that the Pacific performed impressively throughout the trials, its superior steam-producing capacity clearly showing up the deficiencies of the elderly 'Kings', which had themselves been turning in some creditable performances on the 'Cornish Riviera'.

The year 1956 saw the next major change in the appearance of the train. Increased regional autonomy enabled the WR to paint the coaches of its prestige trains in brown and cream livery and to return to lined green livery for any locomotive which could remotely be classed as a 'passenger' train type. Thus, even the diminutive '14xx' 0-4-2Ts started to appear in lined green.

The painting of coaches in regional colours was restricted to fixed rakes of Mk 1 stock for certain named trains, plus one or two ex-GWR restaurant cars required for these services and a handful of slip-coaches. Each of the two sets required for the 'CRE' was marshalled as follows: brake second, three corridor seconds, restaurant second, restaurant kitchen first, corridor first, composite, brake second (all for Penzance), corridor second and brake composite (from Plymouth on up 'CRE' only, down on 11.30am ex-Paddington), with two seconds and a brake second spare. These latter vehicles formed the Penzance portion on summer Saturdays when the main portion of the down train went through to St Ives. This aspect of the service is covered in a separate chapter.

The coaches were painted in brown and cream, reminiscent of GWR livery but not using identical shades. They were lined in standard BR yellow and black and carried the newly-devised coaching stock roundel. The roofboards were in brown and cream with a new style of seriffed italic lettering and the train reverted to the 'Cornish Riviera Limited' title.

A new style of locomotive headboard was also introduced at about this time and was a much more elaborate affair. The cast board was wider and less deep than its predecessor and carried the words 'Cornish Riviera Limited' in seriffed capital letters. An alternative version bore the 'Cornish Riviera Express' title. It was surmounted by the county crest of Cornwall in full colour, the cast board itself being painted cream with brown lettering. All the principal WR expresses were similarly treated, some with even more elaborate headboards. They looked particularly splendid on the top lamp bracket of a gleaming 'King' at the head of a rake of stock in the new livery.

For a short spell in 1956 LMR Pacifics were drafted into the Region to deputise for the 'Kings' which had been temporarily withdrawn due to suspect front bogies following the fracture of one example in January. This substitution lasted only while the remainder of the class were checked for weld failures.

Following the trials with *City of Bristol*, 'King' No 6015 *King Richard III* had been fitted with a double chimney to improve draughting and underwent tests on the 'Cornish Riviera'. Performance was considerably improved and on several occasions senior WR personnel logged the locomotive at over 100mph. In 1956 No 6002 was similarly modified and further members of the class were so treated as they went through works, until in 1958 the first of the diesel-electrics entered traffic and further development work on steam locomotives ceased.

Top left:
A 'scratch' rake of stock including ex-GWR vehicles, Mk 1s newly finished in maroon, and a brown and cream Mk 1 restaurant car, forms the up Sunday working of the 'Cornish Riviera Express' passing Saltash behind 'Warship' No D839 *Relentless* on 29 April 1962.
Brian Haresnape

Above left:
In the late 1960s the 'Cornish Riviera' was again accelerated, a normal 10-coach formation being worked by a pair of 2,200hp 'Warships' operating in multiple. Here, Nos D823 *Hermes* and D870 *Zulu* sprint through Slough with the up train on 11 June 1969. Both wear the maroon livery. *J. H. Cooper-Smith*

Left:
The days of the 'Warship' class were already numbered when the pairings were introduced and those in the best mechanical condition were often in the worst external order. A tatty No D869 *Zest* in maroon livery, leads No D807 *Caradoc*, in blue, down the east side of Dainton on 14 July 1969. With headboard and coach side boards abandoned, the 'Cornish Riviera' is all but anonymous.
G. F. Gillham

Above:
In their early years the 'Westerns' were not widely photographed on the 'Cornish Riviera' and the 'Warships' still shared duties on the train. In later years, however, the 'Westerns' were expected to maintain the exacting schedules developed for the much more powerful 'Warship' pairs. Here, still looking smart in original maroon livery, No D1007 *Western Talisman* heads the blue and grey coaches of the down 'Riviera' towards Twyford on 17 April 1969. *G. P. Cooper*

The diesel era dawned on the Western Region in 1958 with the appearance of the first North British Type 4 diesel-hydraulic No D600 *Active*. One of only five of its kind, the class were really something of a cul-de-sac in the Western Region's dieselisation. The heavy, 12-wheel design, resulting from the BR Board's insistence on the use of slow-running diesel engines, was not really what the Region wanted. Shortly afterwards, No D800 *Sir Brian Robertson*, was delivered. Based on a West German design, with lightweight construction, quick-running engines and only eight wheels, this was the design for which the Western Region was waiting. Like the earlier engines, the majority of these were named after famous British Naval vessels and were known as the 'Warship' class. From the moment of their introduction both heavy and lightweight 'Warships' were used on the 'Cornish Riviera', No D800 wearing a separate headboard proclaiming it as the first 2,200hp diesel-hydraulic to enter traffic. Both diesel types continued to carry the elaborate steam-era headboard, which looked surprisingly well set just below the windscreens.

Cornwall was the first part of the WR to be completely dieselised, but by 1960 the 'Cornish Riviera' was already being exclusively diesel-worked, although steam banking was sometimes provided in South Devon. The light axle-loading of both the 'Warship' classes enabled them to work throughout to Penzance, but while the D800 series assumed exclusivity on the 'Riviera', the D600s were soon relegated to local work within Cornwall, seldom venturing east of Plymouth.

In the early 1960s the coaching stock colour changed again, the use of dedicated rakes for prestige trains preventing more intensive diagramming of the stock. Accordingly, all regions were to paint their coaches in the LMR style of lined maroon. The Southern, however, managed to cling to its green throughout. In reality this simply meant the disappearance of the brown and cream vehicles, for Eastern and Scottish regions had gone straight from carmine and cream to maroon, as had the LMR. By now slip working had ceased, and although it retained its cream headboards, the maroon-liveried 'Cornish Riviera' had started to look like any other WR train.

With the appearance of the more powerful 2,700hp 'Western' class diesel-hydraulics during 1962 the 'Cornish Riviera' took another step towards anonymity, for the 'Westerns' were not equipped to wear the headboard, having no centre lamp bracket. They were fitted with a new-style headboard mounting arrangement, but the headboards to accompany it never went into service.

From the early 1960s the 'Cornish Riviera' included a portion for the Torbay line, which was detached during a stop at Newton Abbot, thus increasing the Paddington-Plymouth time to 4hr 15min with stops also at Taunton and Exeter. 'Westerns' had charge of the train from 1964, but apart from its four-character headcode carried on the front indicator of the locomotive, the 'Cornish Riviera' was becoming less noticeable. The next stage was the replacement of the carriage roof boards by Continental-style name and destination boards at waist level, attached to ugly little metal clips. The most awful feature of the new plates was the use of

Right:
Representing what must be an all time low for a summer 'Cornish Riviera', Brush Type 4 diesel-electric No 1611 heads just six Mk 2 coaches near St Stephens on 23 June 1973. *C. Plant*

Right:
After the abandonment of headboards, the four-character headcode became the easiest way to identify the 'Cornish Riviera' at a distance, though in later years the headcodes were frequently incorrect. The down train had originally been 1C30 but became 1C45 and then 1B45 when all West Country trains adopted the Bristol code. 'Western' No D1058 *Western Nobleman* makes a fine sight bursting out of Parson's Tunnel on to the Teignmouth sea wall on 8 August 1975. *B. Morrison*

black lettering on a yellow background which clashed horribly with the colour of the coaches.

In 1966 a special high-speed working with a 'Western' proved the potential for accelerating West of England services. Two years later, with the axe now hanging over the Western Region's 'non-standard' diesel-hydraulic fleet, the introduction of regular-interval working with 10- and 12-coach trains saw a brief revival for the 'Warships'. Eight locomotives were coupled to form four 4,400hp pairs operating in multiple. They worked the 'Cornish Riviera' and 'Golden Hind' services with a Paddington-Plymouth running time of 3hr 45min and an average speed of over 72mph to Taunton.

The promotional potential of the exercise was largely lost because the trains were now all but anonymous, other than in the timetable, while the locomotives selected for the pairs were in a variety of liveries including the original green, and superseded maroon, and were frequently observed in appallingly shabby condition. What could have been a prestige exercise with locomotives and stock reliveried in 'corporate image' blue, was wasted.

It is doubtful whether any other express has its own stained glass church window, but on 4 May 1969 the 'Cornish Riviera's' 65th anniversary was marked with a service beneath the 'Riviera' window in St James's Church, Sussex Gardens, Paddington. Next day Nos D819 *Goliath* and D808 *Centaur* took the 'Cornish Riviera' to Plymouth in 3hr 23min including a stop at Exeter.

Withdrawals of 'Warships' were now proceeding rapidly and despite severe difficulties in keeping time on the fast schedule without the 4,400hp pairs of 'Warships', 'Westerns' and Brush Type 4 diesel-electrics were increasingly being diagrammed for the 'Cornish Riviera'. The 'Limited' returned to the train's title once more in 1970 as the accommodation was restricted to nine coaches and the Paddington-Plymouth time cut to 3½hr.

The demise of the 'Warships' was followed, in 1972, by the introduction of air-braked Mk 2 coaching stock on the 'Cornish Riviera' which now took the 11.30am departure time from Paddington. The train was becoming increasingly a Brush Type 4 (Class 47) turn. Three years later the 'Westerns' were completely displaced by Class 50 diesel-electrics transferred from the LMR and the 'Cornish Riviera' turned over to Mk 2 air-conditioned coaches. By now, with four-character headcodes also abandoned, the only distinguishing feature of the 'Cornish Riviera' was the paper label stuck inside the droplight of each door.

To mark the passing of locomotive haulage, the last Class 50-worked 'Cornish Riviera' actually carried a commemorative headboard, but otherwise its period of locomotive haulage was ended with a whimper.

With the 75th anniversary of the 'Cornish Riviera' at the start of the 1979 summer timetable, all principal West of England services became worked by IC125 high speed trains. Futher reductions in journey times have followed, but though the fixed formation of the IC125 units means that it is still very much a limited accommodation service, the number of stops is now the same as most other West of England expresses. Nevertheless, in the 1987 timetable, the 'Cornish Riviera' now reaches Plymouth in just 2hr 55min including an Exeter stop, while Penzance is just under 5hr from London, with eight intermediate stops in the Principality. Departure time from Paddington has shifted to 10.50 on weekdays, and 10.45 on Sundays when the train travels via the 'Great Way Round' and includes stops at Reading and Bristol Temple Meads. The rapid acceleration of these trains also means that extra stops can be introduced without incurring a huge time penalty. Weekdays and Saturdays the train still uses the Berks and Hants route, calling only at Exeter St Davids before Plymouth and principal Cornish stations.The Sunday train makes no call at St Erth station as there is no Sunday service on the branch to St Ives.

Below:
The electrification of the Crewe-Glasgow section released English Electric Class 50 locomotives which were transferred to the Western Region from 1975 in order to enable withdrawal of the last 'Western' diesel-hydraulics. The 50s, with their ugly, sad 'expression', were nameless and unkempt when they arrived on the WR and here No 50027 is seen on the up 'Cornish Riviera' at Grafton on 13 October 1975. *D. E. Canning*

Right:
Nearing the end of its career, 'Western' No D1030 *Western Musketeer* brings the up 'Cornish Riviera' off the Berks & Hants line and into Reading station on 7 April 1976. By this time, even the four-character headcodes had passed out of use and the locomotive displays a row of anonymous zeros. *B. Morrison*

Today's 'Cornish Riviera' has a proud tradition and demonstrates the continued improvement in travel times to the West of England. In 80 years, continual refinement has lopped more than an hour off the time to Plymouth and another half hour off the difficult Cornish stretch. The impact of private motoring and ultra-cheap high-speed motorway coaches have taken their toll of the West Country traffic — particularly summer holiday traffic. Despite valiant attempts to win back traffic with services such as Motorail, the railway has not really been successful in attempts to regain traffic on the route. One has only to compare the eight-coach IC125 'Cornish Riviera' with the mammoth 14-coach train of the steam era (with relief workings too) to see just how the traffic has dwindled.

Nevertheless, where the railway has enjoyed increased traffic it has done so by the medium of faster and faster services. That tradition, like the tradition of seaside holidays in Cornwall, is due in no small measure to the 'Cornish Riviera' express.

Above left:
The last locomotive-hauled up weekday 'Cornish Riviera' approaches Castle Cary behind Class 50 No 50047 *Swiftsure* on 4 August 1979. With the exception of the luggage and refreshment vehicles, the train is formed of Mk 2 air-conditioned stock. *John A. M. Vaughan*

Left:
Whilst enabling another significant acceleration of the service, the IC125 units, with their fixed formation of coaches, have again brought the 'Cornish Riviera' to the status of a limited accommodation service. The down train is here seen on Wrangaton Bank, near Ivybridge, on 10 July 1980. *B. Morrison*

Slip Coaches

Right:
The Great Western Railway was Britain's largest user of the system of slipping coaches, which enabled vehicles to be detached from a moving train to serve places en route without stopping the main train. The system's major disadvantages were that passengers in slip coaches did not have access to the rest of the train for refreshments etc, and that the system only worked in one direction — return services had to stop in order to attach coaches. Nevertheless, at its height the 'Cornish Riviera' conveyed three separate slip portions. This end view of a Toplight 'Concertina' slip coach shows the special hinged coupling hook, self-sealing pipes, warning bell and windows to the slip guard's compartment. *GWR/Ian Allan Library*

Below:
The final slip coaches on the Western Region were conversions of postwar Hawksworth brake composites and were among the few ex-GWR design coaches to receive the brown and cream livery to match the Mk 1 stock on principal services. The vehicle seen here is coasting into Didcot after slipping from the 7.00am Weston-super-Mare–Paddington. *J. A. Coiley*

Left:
A view inside the slip compartment, showing the large handbrake standard (white) and to its right the lever which operates the hinged coupling hook to detach the slip coach from the train.
GWR/Ian Allan Library

Below:
The main portion of the 'Cornish Riviera' draws away from the slip coach after slipping at Heywood Junction near Westbury. The slip portion was taken into Westbury by an 0-6-0PT and attached to the next Weymouth train. *H. C. Casserley*

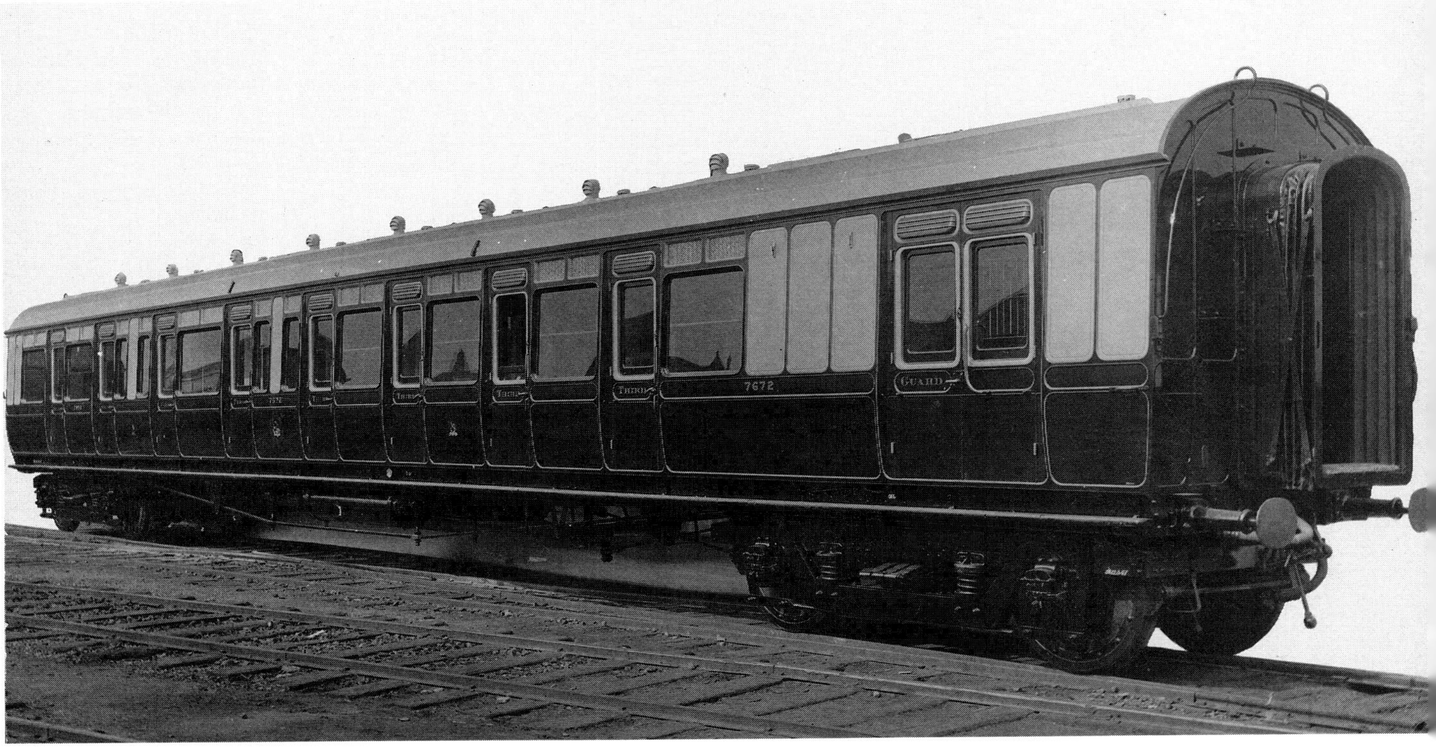

7776

CORNISH RIVIERA EXPRESS
9582
THIRD CLASS
G W R
RESTAURANT CAR
FIRST CLASS
9582

Coaching Stock

Top left:
The doors of the wide-bodied 70ft Toplight coaches built in 1906/7 were recessed in order to bring the door handles within the loading gauge, giving the curious 'concertina' effect. This is brake composite No 7672 of 1907.
GWR/Ian Allan Library

Centre left:
Toplight 70ft corridor composite No 7776 finished in the chocolate lake livery and photographed on 13 September 1920.
GWR/Ian Allan Library

Bottom left:
Composite 1st/3rd class restaurant car No 9582 of the 1929-built bow-ended stock for the 'Cornish Riviera Express'.
GWR/Ian Allan Library

Right:
The interior of a typical third class compartment in the 1929 stock.
GWR/Ian Allan Library

Below:
'Centenary' third class restaurant car No 9637 of 1935. The wide body again necessitated recessed doors, but even so the vehicles were banned from certain lines, as indicated on the solebar.
GWR/Ian Allan Library

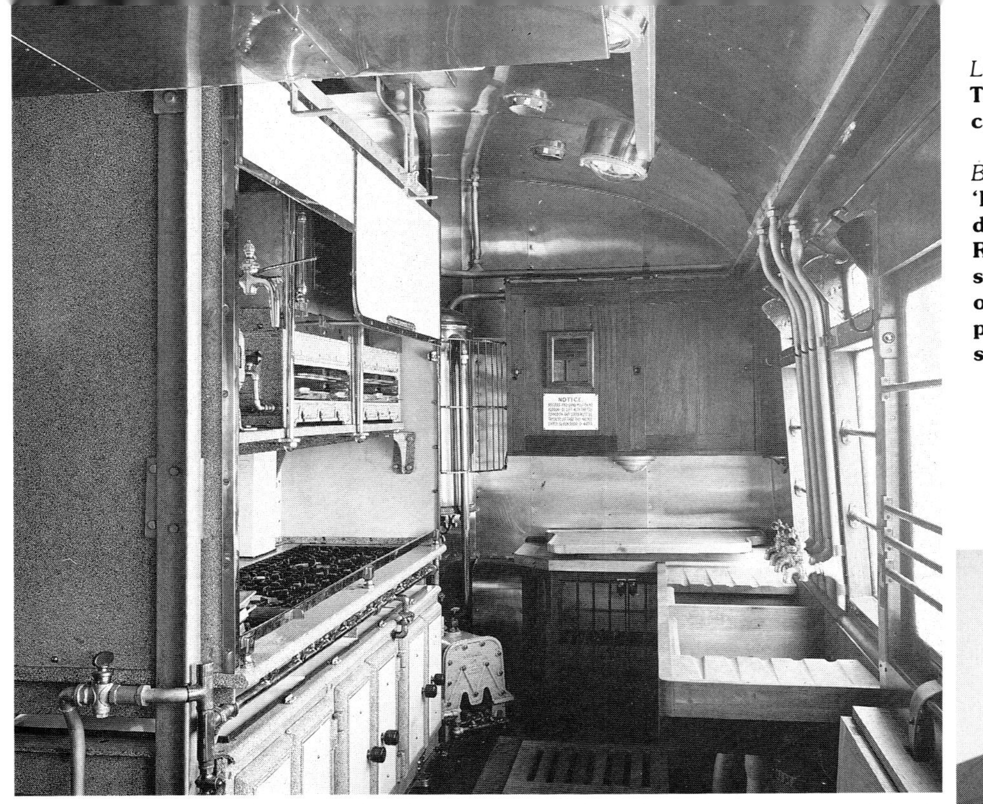

Left:
The kitchen of a 'Centenary' restaurant car. *GWR/Ian Allan Library*

Below:
'King' No 6020 *King Henry IV* heads the down 'Cornish Riviera Express' past Reading locomotive depot. The coaching stock is the Hawksworth postwar pattern of 1946 in the final GWR livery. Note the placing of the roof boards on this and subsequent BR stock. *M. W. Earley*

Left:
The interior of a third class compartment in the 1946 stock. *GWR/Ian Allan Library*

CHAPTER FIVE

Summer Saturday service to St Ives

Above:
On 26 July 1958 '45xx' 2-6-2Ts Nos 4547/66 wait in the up siding at St Erth with the Paddington-St Ives portion of the 'Cornish Riviera', delayed 65min awaiting a path over the branch.
P. Q. Treloar

The 4 mile 22 chain branch from St Ives Road (later St Erth) to St Ives was opened as a broad gauge line on 1 June 1877. It was the last broad gauge branch line built, and was worked from the outset by the South Devon Railway, until absorbed by the GWR on 1 August 1878.

At St Erth, the branch connects with the main line in the Penzance direction, and is served by a bay platform behind, and slightly below, the up platform. After passing through the up sidings at St Erth, the single track diverges to run along the Hayle estuary to the small platform and wooden building at Lelant (1 mile 5 chains). From here it faces a steady climb at 1 in 60 to gain its cliff-top position at Carbis Bay (2 miles 78 chains), continuing to climb around Porthminster Point, where a short level stretch is reached before the 1 in 60 descent into St Ives station.

In steam days there was a 30mph speed restriction throughout the branch, with a 15mph restriction from the stop board on Porthminster Point down into St Ives. Motive power variety was also restricted and in later years the small prairies of the '45xx' series were used almost exclusively. A single locomotive was permitted a load of 190 tons, or 220 tons if 1 min extra running time was allowed.

Right:
St Erth station in August 1958. Nos 4540/66 are starting away over the crossover with the down 'Cornish Riviera' to St Ives. 'Manor' No 7814 *Fringford Manor* (left) has charge of the three-coach Penzance portion. *P. Q. Treloar*

Below right:
A panoramic view of Porthminster beach at St Ives on 1 August 1953. The down 'Cornish Riviera' is just arriving at St Ives, the leading locomotive having been detached and run on to the engine siding. Its smoke is visible in the trees above the golf course. The third locomotive, required to move the empty stock out of the station stands by the water tank, visible above the rear of the train. *B. A. Butt*

Carbis Bay had a staffed station, with its booking hall at street level and the platform below in a cutting. The latter boasted only a small waiting shelter, built of red brick and almost identical to the one at Colnbrook, just near my home. Opposite the platform the station name was emblazoned across the grass bank in whitewashed stones, interspersed with flowers. There were no sidings then, and it appeared that there never had been.

The station site at St Ives was equally cramped because of its position on a ledge part way up the cliff. Down trains descending the final gradient into the station, first passed the single-road engine shed on the left, with its stone-built coaling stage and large water tank outside. They then crossed a low viaduct — so low that from most angles it is scarcely visible. It was a series of lattice girder spans on stone piers, but sometime around 1960 the lattice spans were replaced with the present plate girders. Beyond the viaduct the run-round loop diverged, together with two sidings, one serving the small stone goods shed and the other forming a bay behind the passenger platform. These were the only goods facilities provided, which is surprising in view of the heavy fish traffic which once originated here. In later years the siding housed a camping coach during summer months. The platform was capable of accommodating up to about 10 coaches and both platform line and run-round ended in long headshunts which were frequently choked with spare coaches. These would be added to trains in the morning and evening peaks and removed after about 10.30am in order to reduce the trains to two or three coaches. There was thus activity either adding or removing coaches during much of the day.

The branch was worked by electric train staff between St Erth Junction and St Ives, with no intermediate crossing places. For much of the day there would be at least one locomotive on shed being coaled and watered ready to take out the next train, after carrying out any necessary shunting movements. The locomotive from the incoming train would then take its place on shed, after providing banking assistance up the incline if the train was a heavy one.

The 'Cornish Riviera' service included a stop at St Erth to connect with services to and from St Ives, but on summer Saturdays, at least during the 1950s, the main portion of the train operated through to St Ives, with a small section being detached at St Erth to go forward to Penzance. The St Ives through service was provided only by the down 'Cornish Riviera', the corresponding up working, the 9.20am off St Ives, being un-named. This train seems to have been typical of summer Saturday workings to and from the Cornish branches, in being made up of older coaches and certainly lacking the prestige of the 'Cornish Riviera'. In the up direction it left St Ives at 9.20am, arriving St Erth at 9.35am, where it would run into the up main platform to reverse, the branch 2-6-2Ts being replaced with a main line locomotive backing on to the rear of the train. Arrival in London was scheduled for 4.40pm. It called at Carbis Bay and Lelant and was available for local travel, those travelling beyond Plymouth being required to hold the customary Seat Regulation tickets, which were designed to enable the pressure on West of England main line services to be assessed in advance. The down 'Cornish Riviera' to St Ives was timetabled for a 10.30am departure from Paddington, the normal weekday timing for the Penzance train. It reached St Erth at 5.15pm and a pair of 2-6-2Ts would then take it on over the branch with a 5.35pm arrival in St Ives. The stock appears to have then formed the 5.45pm departure for St Erth although this working was allowed only the customary 15 min to traverse the branch. In comparison, the 8.40am ex-St Erth which brought in the stock for the up train was allowed 2 min extra running time.

I well remember seeing the down 'Cornish Riviera' at St Ives on several occasions. Its immaculate rake of BR Mk 1

coaches in brown and cream could scarcely have passed unnoticed, particularly since it filled the station to capacity.

The train normally consisted of a 10-coach rake, the other three or four vehicles having gone on to Penzance behind the engine which had brought them from Plymouth. At St Erth two '45xx' 2-6-2Ts would be attached to the rear of the train and would then draw it across the main line and on to the branch. There were no booked stops at the branch stations, and arrival at St Ives was at 5.35pm. The station platform was required to be clear through to the stop blocks, and one '45xx' on shed. When the train arrived at St Ives Inner Home signal it would be stopped and the leading locomotive detached. This locomotive would then join the one on shed and the remaining locomotive would then gently ease the train downgrade into the station. With this locomotive tight up against the stop blocks the train could just be accommodated in the platform. The locomotive would then be uncoupled in readiness to bank the train out of the station, while the two locomotives from the shed would double-head the return working. The banking engine would then remain at St Ives to head the next up local train. It must have been one of few small country branch lines to regularly witness three locomotives working a single train.

We frequently stayed at the Headlands Hotel, above Porthminster Point and well on the way to Carbis Bay. A footpath provided quick access to the beach and also paralleled the railway, crossing it in at least one place. Returning to the hotel one Saturday afternoon, as we reached the bridge we heard the 5.45pm making its departure from St Ives. I was 12 years old. I swung my brand new Kodak Brownie 44A over the parapet, but the view westwards was full into the sun. As the train passed underneath, I did manage a rear three-quarter view of the two '45xxs' storming up through the rock cutting, working flat out, a third of their kind pushing hard in the rear.

Above left:
Two unrecorded '45xx' 2-6-2Ts head the empty stock of the down 'Cornish Riviera' away from St Ives, banked in the rear by a third member of the class.
Author

Above right:
'Grange' 4-6-0 No 6873 *Caradoc Grange* waits to work the empty stock of the down 'Cornish Riviera' from St Erth to Penzance for stabling on 4 July 1958.
P. Q. Treloar

In May 1966 I was able to renew acquaintance with the branch after several years' absence, thanks to the non-stop Paddington-Penzance rail tour organised by Ian Allan Ltd. It was reminiscent of the various high-speed trials of earlier years and it was to confound the sceptics who said that the Western Region could not run a train from one end of its system to the other without stopping it somewhere en route! The trip allowed sufficient time after arrival at Penzance for us to take in a trip to St Ives.

By this time Gloucester single-unit railcars had taken over from the NBL Type 2 diesels which heralded the end of steam on the branch in 1961. Any possibility of through main line workings had gone. At St Ives all the buildings were intact, although only a single track remained, cut short in the length of the platform. Subsequently over several years, the site was systematically cleared for car parking, and a new, ugly little station built at the end of the viaduct.

For the time being though, only the motive power had changed, and I was privileged to enjoy a cab ride back to St Erth. The grandeur of the scenery and the splendid views out across the wild Atlantic could still be appreciated, and, happily, they still can be, whatever the motive power. This is *real* 'Cornish Riviera' country.

Right:
The balancing working in the up direction was not strictly part of the 'Cornish Riviera', merely the 9.20am (SO) St Ives-Paddington. On 4 July 1959 Nos 4564/71 head the train formed of mixed ex-GWR stock, along the Hayle Estuary near Lelant. *P. Q. Treloar*

Out of Course

Right:
Drainage work on the West of England line caused extensive diversions in 1951 and the Sunday down 'Cornish Riviera' ran via Bath and Bristol. Usually it was 'King'-hauled, but on 11 November 1951 'County' No 1024 *County of Pembroke* had charge of the train as it passed Tilehurst in the Thames Valley.
M. W. Earley

Below:
During these diversions, the weekday 'Cornish Riviera' ran via Swindon and Melksham to regain the West of England route. 'Castle' No 5035 *Coity Castle* has just passed Thingley Junction, Chippenham on 17 October 1951.
G. J. Jefferson

Bottom:
'King' No 6013 *King Henry VIII* heads the down Sunday 'Cornish Riviera' past West Thingley, Chippenham, on 3 May 1953, diverted from its usual route due to bridge repairs. *G. J. Jefferson*

Top:
In one of the 1955 dynamometer car test runs, the locomotive featured in the previous illustration, No 6013, heads the down 'Cornish Riviera' on its usual route, near Reading West. The Churchward dynamometer car No W7W is the first vehicle in the train. *M. W. Earley*

Above left:
As part of the same series of trials Stanier 'Duchess' 4-6-2 No 46237 *City of Bristol* was borrowed for comparison purposes. Again, the viewpoint is near Reading West. *M. W. Earley*

Left:
Piloting over the South Devon banks was normal for all but the lightest trains. Here, the 'Duchess' receives a hand from an unrecorded 'Castle', the pair going in fine style. *D. S. Fish*

Right, top to bottom:
From time to time incursions by the sea along the South Devon coast, and other problems on this difficult route, would necessitate diversions. At that time the Southern route from Plymouth via Okehampton to Exeter provided a useful alternative and on 26 August 1961, 'Warship' No D867 *Zenith* was photographed passing Meldon Junction with the 10.00 Penzance-Paddington, up 'Cornish Riviera'. Reversal would be required at Exeter St Davids to regain the WR route. *S. C. Nash*

The down 'Cornish Riviera' enters Westbury station with 'Warship' No D824 *Highflyer* in disgrace. It is a wintry 6 November 1960 and the 'Warship's' train steam heating boiler has broken down, so a call is being made to collect a steam locomotive pilot for the rest of the journey. *A. Hobbs*

The up 'Cornish Riviera', behind an unrecorded 'Western' diesel-hydraulic, passes Hawkeridge Junction, Westbury, diverted via Bradford Junction and Chippenham due to Sunday engineering work on the Berks & Hants line.
J. H. Sparkes

An unusual diversion finds 'Western' No D1039 *Western King* in heavy rain on the outskirts of Salisbury with the down 'Cornish Riviera' on 6 July 1969. The train was running via Reading, Basingstoke and the SR route to Exeter to avoid a derailment which had occurred two days earlier at Stoke Canon.
Ian Allan Library

Far right, top:
A cavalcade passes Lavington on 24 October 1978. Class 50 No 50025 *Invincible* (left), heading the down 'Cornish Riviera', assists No 50047 *Swiftsure* (right) on the 10.55 Paddington-Paignton, after the latter had suffered an engine room fire.
D. E. Canning

Far right, bottom:
Diverted due to resignalling work, the down 'Cornish Riviera' formed by IC125 unit No 253.036, is seen three miles east of Warminster on 4 January 1981.
D. E. Canning

Locomotives

Above:
Perhaps more than any other class, the mighty 'King' 4-6-0s were most associated with the 'Cornish Riviera Express'. Even 'Kings' were provided with assistance between Newton Abbot and Plymouth over the South Devon banks. In July 1950, 'Manor' No 7805 *Broome Manor* was photographed piloting No 6002 *King William IV* on the climb to Dainton Summit.
H. Gordon Tidey

Centre right:
'Kings' were not permitted beyond the Saltash Bridge, so more lowly classes often worked the 'Cornish Riviera' between Penzance and Plymouth. Waiting at the terminus with the up train is 'Hall' 4-6-0 No 5964 *Wolseley Hall*, immaculately turned out in BR mixed traffic lined black livery. With the 1946 coaches finished in carmine and cream livery the train must have made a fine sight. *P. Ransome-Wallis*

Right:
On a very dull 15 February 1952 the down 'Cornish Riviera' is hustled through Iver by 'Castles' Nos 5012 *Berry Pomeroy Castle* and 5023 *Brecon Castle*. Double-heading in this fashion was unusual and probably just for convenience of locomotive working. *B. Morrison*

Above:
The only Pacifics to find regular use on the 'Cornish Riviera' were the BR standard 'Britannias', and then they were usually confined to the Plymouth-Penzance section. The down train is seen arriving at Gwinear Road station, junction of the branch to Helston. The approaching branch train is visible above the third coach. The date is 10 April 1952. *B. A. Butt*

Left:
The big NBL 'Warships' were handsome machines and looked fine at the head of the brown and cream stock, although the offset lamp bracket meant that the headboard position was rather strange. The first of the class, No D600 *Active* was at the head of the up train at Penzance station on 5 June 1958. It had entered traffic only four months earlier.
P. Thatcher

Top right:
The D800-series 'Warships' were derived from a German design and the first of the class was named after BTC Chairman, *Sir Brian Robertson*. They quickly displaced the larger machines from prestige duties, and on 2 October 1958 No D800 is seen crossing Hayle Causeway with the down 'Cornish Riviera Express'. The front of this design was later modified to incorporate a four-character headcode display in place of the discs. *B. A. Butt*

Centre right:
A wintry panorama of Reading on 5 March 1970 as 'Warship' multiple-unit pair Nos D824 *Highflyer* and D819 *Goliath* sprint towards London with the up 'Cornish Riviera'. Both locomotives wear slightly different versions of the blue livery which did not suit their rounded styling. *G. P. Cooper*

Below:
The 'Western' diesel-hydraulics came into their own on the 'Cornish Riviera' for a few short years in the early 1970s, in blue livery with early Mk 2 coaches. Epitomising that era, No D1010 *Western Campaigner* heads the down 'Cornish Riviera' away from Paddington on 25 April 1973. *B. Morrison*

Top left:
A defective indicator blind adds to the anonymity of the down 'Cornish Riviera' as Brush Type 4 (later Class 47) No 1750 races through Sonning Cutting on 27 April 1974. *B. Morrison*

Centre left:
The final locomotive class to have regular duty on the 'Cornish Riviera' were the English Electric Class 50s, drafted in from the LMR where they had worked prestige trains such as the 'Royal Scot'. No 50038 *Formidable* (the second of its name on the WR) scowls for the camera as it passes Reading West with the 11.30am Paddington-Penzance 'Cornish Riviera' on 5 June 1978. *I. J. Hodson*

Below:
Though aesthetically little more than a glorified diesel multiple-unit, the IC125s offer comfort and speed consistent with the long tradition of the 'Cornish Riviera'. Unit No 253.017 forms the down train approaching Castle Cary on 29 August 1979, shortly before the schedules were further accelerated.
J. R. Acton

Penzance

Top:
Penzance station is in a seafront location which always seems to be basking in glorious sunshine, lending real 'Riviera' atmosphere to an arrival by train. This delightful view on 9 July 1953 shows 'Hall' No 6949 *Haberfield Hall* waiting at the head of the up 'Cornish Riviera'. In the background, the curved timber frontage of the trainshed has since been removed. Note, too, the slip coach (not in use as a slip vehicle) on the rear of the adjacent train. *C. R. L. Coles*

Above right:
'Castle' No 5058 *Earl of Clancarty* rests inside Penzance station after bringing the down 'Cornish Riviera' from Plymouth on 10 September 1952.
L. Overend

Right:
From Penzance passengers can travel onward to the beautiful Isles of Scilly, either by the mv *Scillonian* with daily sailings from Penzance harbour, or by helicopter as seen in this view of a British Airways Sea King landing at the heliport adjacent to Long Rock carriage sidings.
L. Bertram

Below:
The crew of BR Standard 'Britannia' 4-6-2 No 70019 *Lightning* really put their backs into turning the locomotive at Ponsandane depot, Penzance, after arrival with the down 'Cornish Riviera' on 26 April 1952. The locomotive was booked to return to Plymouth on the 7.30pm departure. *B. A. Butt*

Bottom:
The year 1966 saw various experimental runs to the West Country in connection with potential service improvements: an indirect spin-off was the operation of a non-stop Paddington-Penzance special for Publisher Ian Allan. A fast non-stop down run with 'Western' power was eclipsed by the return Plymouth-Waterloo section behind 'Warship' No D823 *Hermes*. This was the scene at Penzance on the day. A local from Plymouth has arrived (right) as the excursion stands stabled (left) beyond the Swindon Cross-Country DMU. *Author*

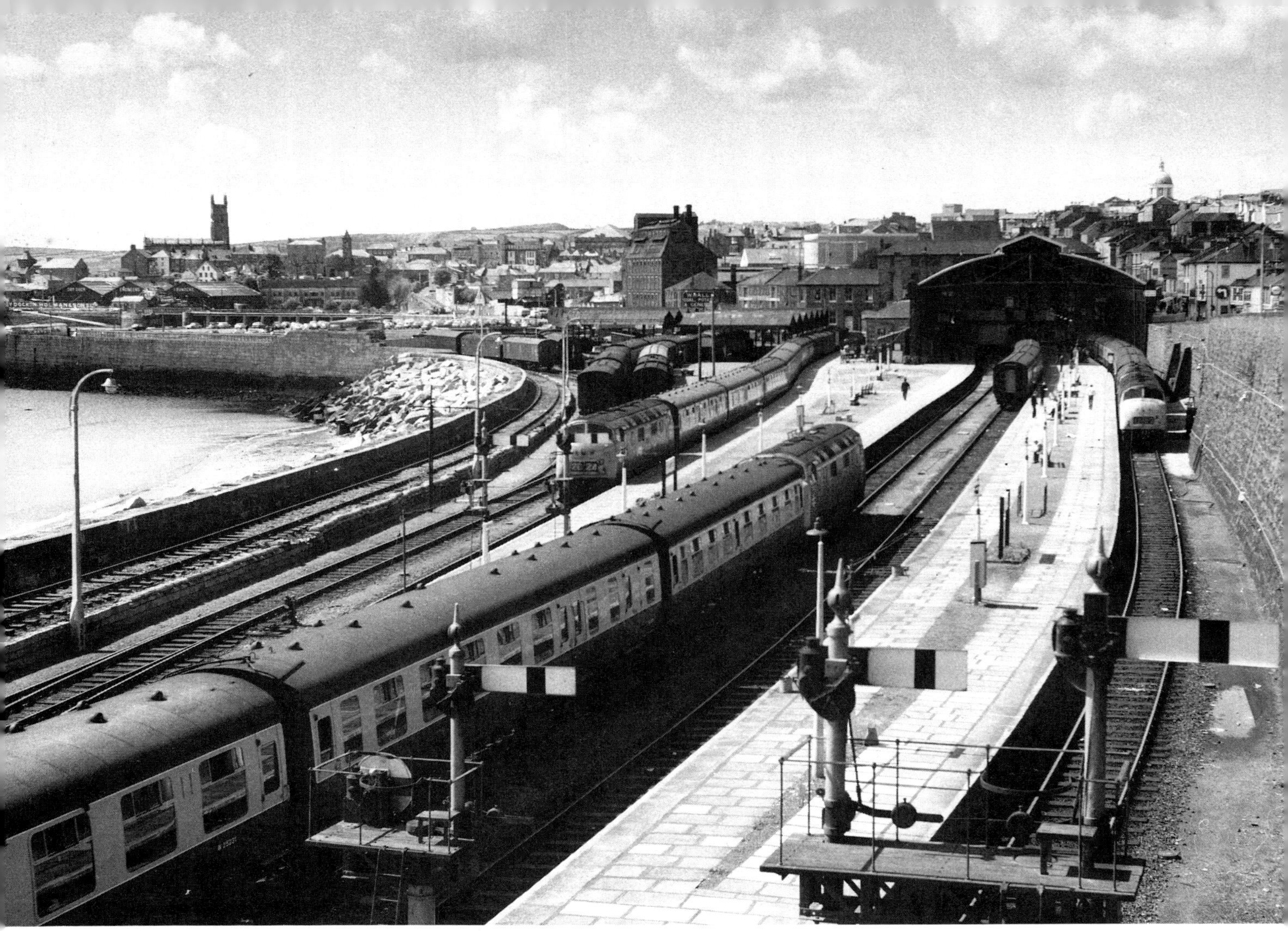

Above:
A panorama of Penzance in the 'Warship' era. On the left may be seen the dry dock and the road leading towards Newlyn harbour and Mousehole. A down express is arriving while an up local waits to depart and a third 'Warship' marshalls parcels vans. The date is May 1968.
G. F. Heiron

Right:
Not the Royal Train, but the down 'Cornish Riviera' incorrectly displaying two tail lamps as it passes the site of Savernake station on 27 July 1978.
D. E. Canning